DEAL WITH DEBT in 90 Minutes

Graham Willmott

Illustrations by Ama Page

ll.

2000

Every effort has been made to ensure that the advice given in this book is correct, but the publishers, authors, editors and consultants regret that they cannot accept any liability whatever for errors of omission or commission arising from the use of these notes. The publisher is not in the business of giving (legal or financial) advice or other professional services.

Copyright © Graham Willmott 2004, 2008

First edition published under the title "Forget Debt in 90 Minutes" in 2004
by Management Books 2000 Ltd

This edition first published in 2008 by Management Books 2000 Ltd
Forge House, Limes Road
Kemble, Cirencester
Gloucestershire, GL7 6AD, UK
Tel: 0044 (0) 1285 771441/2
Fax: 0044 (0) 1285 771055
E-mail: info@mb2000.com
Website: www.mb2000.com

British Library Cataloguing in Publication Data is available

ISBN 9781852526009

In Ninety Minutes

For a complete list of Management Books 2000 titles,
visit our web-site on www.mb2000.com

Other titles in The Ninety Minute Series are:

25 Management Techniques in 90 Minutes
5S Kaizen in 90 Minutes
Active Learning in 90 Minutes
Become a Meeting Anarchist in 90 Minutes
Budgeting in 90 Minutes
Building a Website Using a CMS in 90 Minutes
Credit Control in 90 Minutes
Damn Clients! in 90 Minutes
Deal With Debt in 90 Minutes
Effective Media Coverage in 90 Minutes
Emotional Intelligence in 90 Minutes
Faster Promotion in 90 Minutes
Find That Job in 90 Minutes
Funny Business in 90 Minutes
Getting More Visitors to Your Website in 90 Minutes
Learn to Use a PC in 90 Minutes
Networking in 90 Minutes
Payroll in 90 Minutes
Perfect CVs in 90 Minutes
Plan a New Website in 90 Minutes
Practical Negotiating in 90 Minutes
Run a Successful Conference in 90 Minutes
Strengths Coaching in 90 Minutes
Supply Chain in 90 Minutes
Telling People in 90 Minutes
Understand Accounts in 90 Minutes
Working From Home in 90 Minutes
Working Together in 90 Minutes

Contents

Chapter 1 – Introduction 7

1 – Reducing the worry of debt 9
2 – Face up to it, the dangers of ignoring creditors 15
3 – Consolidation loans 21
4 – Existing debts 23

Chapter 2 – Immediate action – starting now 27

1 – Contact your creditors today 29
2 – Positive action 35
3 – Your mortgage/rent – safeguard your home 41
4 – Household services 50
5 – Credit cards 56
6 – Car/equipment loans 58
7 – Student loans 59
8 – Child Support Agency 64

Chapter 3 – Income 65

1 – The DSS 67
2 – Pooling your income 70
3 – Protecting your income 72
4 – Limit your outgoings 75
5 – Money you didn't know you had 77
6 – Tax Credits 80

Chapter 4 – The Law 81

1 – Repossession – voluntary or otherwise 83
2 – Credit cards 88
3 – Bailiffs 93
4 – Harassment 96
5 – Win the court case 99

6 – Interest rates   104
7 – Writing off a debt   105
8 – Little known laws   106
9 – Voluntary arrangements   108
10 – Bankruptcy   111

Chapter 5 – Assistance   **115**
1 – How to get free advice   117
2 – Free legal assistance   119
3 – Insurance   120
4 – Stress and worry free nights   121

Appendix   **123**

Index   **125**

DEAL WITH DEBT
in NINETY MINUTES

Introduction

1

Introduction

1. Reducing the worry of debt

If you owe money to one of the big financial institutions, or perhaps a small company or even an individual, they all have one thing in common. And that is you have something they want and by any principle you wish to apply, that puts you firmly in driving seat. If you are in debt, you should be in charge of it and if you are, it is easy to manage on your own terms. After all, you are the only one who can give your creditors what they want. This book aims to show you how to do just that, and stop worrying about debt.

> To begin with, let us put something into perspective. At the time of publication, the UK National Debt stands at approximately **640 billion** of your hard-earned English pounds. Divide that by the population of this country and it means that every single individual – rich man, poor man woman and child – is responsible for a debt of more than **ten thousand pounds** – each.

Now, hopefully, that puts whatever debt problem *you* have into perspective, so let's start dealing with it.

In recent years, it has been far too easy to slip into unmanageable debt. Everywhere we turn, credit companies have been trying to convince us to borrow and buy, and whenever we ran into trouble, another company would lend to us again, and again, and again. **'Buy now and spread your payments'** or **'Fast free loans'** was the tone of many adverts. Even worse the one that reads:

> **'WORRIED ABOUT DEBT? TAKE OUT A LOAN.'**

That was before the Credit Crunch, of course, when all the lenders suddenly changed their tune! Now it is increasingly hard to borrow money anywhere, and this has created enormous difficulties for a growing number of people who find themselves saddled with debts they cannot renew or extend. This is ample proof of the old adage that banks are like people who sell umbrellas in the sunshine, but ask for them back as soon as it starts raining!

Couple this drying up of the lending market with a lack of real job security – in some cases, the lack of any job at all – and lots of us soon find ourselves in big debt. You are not alone; there are millions of us.

In fact, millions of people are faced with court action or the threat of disconnection or property repossession.

But help is at hand. The following pages will show you how you can begin to work your way out of this dangerous maze...

To start with, your creditors (the people who have lent you money, or sold you products on deferred payment terms) also have some responsibility for your indebtedness – and that is why we mustn't let them have it all their own way.

None of us *want* to lose our homes, cars or bikes. None of us *want* the debt collectors calling around and none of us can relax when the bills and nasty letters are piling up. But is it entirely our fault? The answer is, assuredly, no. We have been encouraged to take on debt beyond our means, and the results are now plain for all to see. The responsibility for this lies squarely with the lenders who went out of their way to encourage unsafe borrowing (and spending).

The important thing to remember, now, is that ***you must not see yourself as a financial failure.***

Start by feeling **positive** about the situation you are in. One thing you can be sure of is that somebody somewhere is deeper in it than you are. Like them, you can get out of it and you have already started.

> You are about to find out all you need to know that will solve your problems and allow you to rest easy and forget about them. More importantly, you will learn in plain English, just how far your creditors can go, what you can do about it, how much you can get away with and how you get started.

The biggest problem many people have is not taking a debt seriously enough and that in itself, as we see later, will cost even more money as our problems pile up. It seems easier to ignore latest reminders, those nasty-looking envelopes that get heaped up in the back of the drawer, or in the back of a bin, than it is to open them and look at what we owe. When we can't afford the gas bill, it lays unopened, but it doesn't stop us worrying about it.

Employing the Ostrich Method of debt management (sticking our heads in the sand and hoping it all goes away) guarantees only one thing – that we lose control of all the events surrounding our finances. The standard letters will continue to pour in and the interest and charges continue to pour out, and *we* let that happen. In short, the ship sails on, only instead of steering it into calmer waters, we find ourselves in deeper ones. That is no way to handle the problem and we will always have the worry of debt in everything we do. And we could lose forever the chance to square our accounts on our own terms and to our own benefit.

Budgeting

In this book we will only be spending a short time on the subject of budgeting. Many books have been written on the subject of good personal financial management, and this is, of course, esential. However, when large cumulative debts have been racked up, there is more to be done than agonising over allocating the £20 a month to petrol or £100 per week on advertising. For the purpose of this book we will concentrate on the immediate task in hand – the reduction of your personal debt. We will explain in this book how to optimise the use of your income, and dramatically reduce your outgoings for the purposes of dealing with the immediate debt problem. And rather than use up space outlining general budgeting principles (which are, in any event, fairly obvious), we will use all the room we have here on direct and factual advice, geared towards coping with the worry of debt and making positive progress towards getting out of it.

Creditors

We will learn how to deal with our creditors whoever they may be. Whilst most creditors differ in their approach, and there are no hard and fast rules for dealing with them, the advice here will be practical, not technical. It illustrates what to look out for, what we are likely to get away with, how we should be approaching our creditors and what we are trying to achieve at every step along the way. There are even standard letters included that can be adapted and sent out and we will find out how to turn a few of the laws around and use them to our own advantage. The very laws our creditors hope we will not find out about.

We will look closely at what has happened to us and put ourselves into a position where our creditors never need bother us again, or in some cases can't touch us. We will begin to deal with them on our own terms and should they continue to bother us they could be breaking the law. They could be the ones in trouble not us.

In future, you will not have to hide from the postman, fearing that dreaded knock on the door that comes with a bill or registered letter. Never again will you ignore the phone, leave the post unopened or hide behind the couch when you hear footsteps on the path.

Today, as of this moment, you are back in control. This book puts you there and keeps you there.

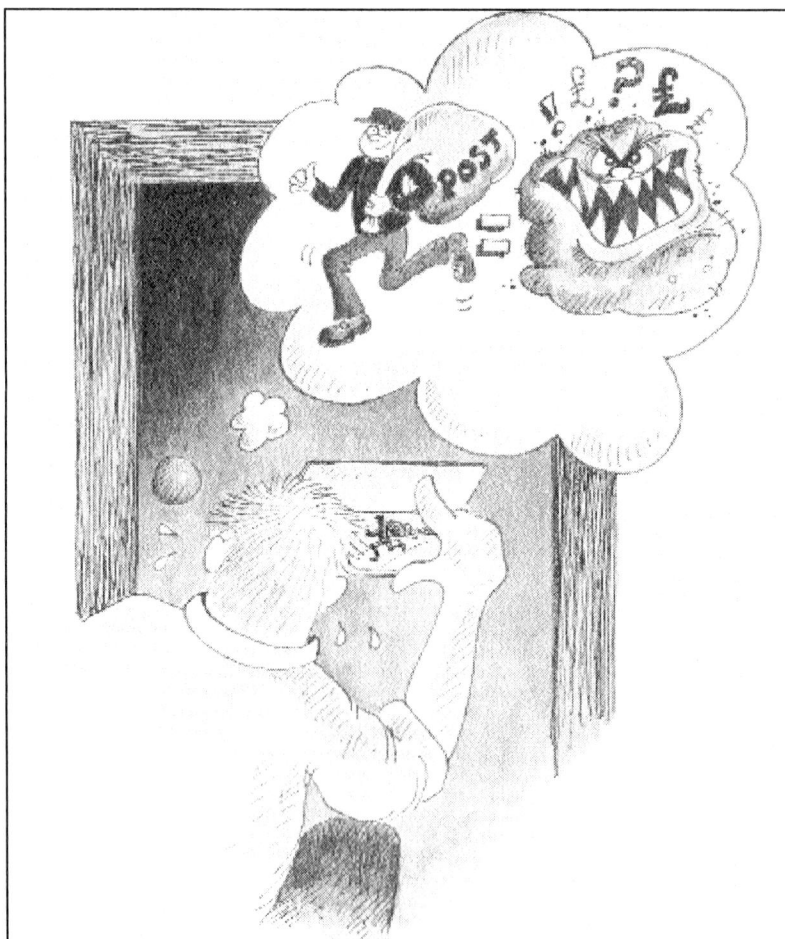

2. Face up to it – the dangers of ignoring creditors

The fact is, you may have some, if not several, outstanding debts, invoices or bills that you simply cannot afford to pay. The single most important task you have is, believe it or not, just to face up to it.

Every bill is catalogued in the human mind in order of either size or importance. A small bill owed to the milkman can be equally as worrying as a £10,000 bank loan, if we know the milkman well. The task of sitting down and listing out your debts, in no particular order, is probably the hardest and most harrowing task on the route to recovery.

The first task is to create a pile of invoices, unseal all those envelopes and have a good look through them. As you work through the pile you are bound to come across the odd few that you don't regard as particularly important – but list them anyway. We do not want anything, however large or small, left outside this programme to worry about. Everything must go in the pot, so to speak, and even if you have been trying to forget all about them, the creditors haven't! Nobody forgets when you owe them money so you can never be completely free from the worry of debt unless you see every single item laid out in front of you, in black and white. Try and walk away from it, and it follows you around.

As you work though the pile, you must make a list of each debt and note the agreed monthly payment, if there is one, alongside the balance. Those that don't have an agreed monthly repayment, such as quarterly bills or an overdraft, should have a space left for a figure to be allocate later. Pretty soon you start to see a picture emerging of the entire debt position and often it isn't as bad as first imagined. It doesn't matter how long the list is, or how small each item is, put them all down.

Example:

Creditors	Total Owed	Monthly Payment
Woolfax Building Society (Mortgage arrears)	£2000	
Textiles U.K.	£1200	£50
Credit card 1	£1100	£65
Bank loan	£5600	£323
Credit card 2	£850	£45
British Telecom	£65	
British Gas	£79	
Car repair	£220	
Newsagent	£15	
Milkman	£22	
Etc.		
	-----------	-----------
Totals	**£11,151**	**£483**

Now start on a second index of all monthly expenses but leave out all the debt repayments. The idea here is to try to reschedule those payments with an new affordable amount so you need to know exactly what is left over from your income that can be allocated to repaying the debt. It may be very little, it may be nothing, but whatever it is, you need to find out. Once again, it doesn't matter how small the item or how long the list is. Put *everything* down with a good estimate against each one that doesn't already have a fixed repayment such as food, petrol, bus fares and clothing.

If income is either weekly or bi-weekly, lists of expenses should be made to correspond those time periods. It's much easier as there are rarely four full weeks in a month, sometimes there are even five, so it is better to list expenses to match income. These figures become your budget, and will double as your **Financial Statement.**

Example:

Expenses	Monthly
Mortgage or Rent	£750
Food	£230
Water rates/community charge	£80
School dinners	£15
Child Care	£25
Clothes	£75
Insurance	£31
Car tax/insurance	£44

Total	**£1250**

Monthly Income	£1550
Balance	£300

Using these examples, it is clear to see there is not enough money from the balance, after all the vital household expenses have been met, to cover the current debt repayments. These household expenses are the most important liabilities we have, so, to keep them to a sensible amount, they should not be compromised in any way by any other creditor. These expenses are regarded as the bare minimum you need to survive and are more important that consumer debts, which will only be paid out of whatever you have left over, however small an amount that is.

Now, looking at our list of debts, it would initially seem that the larger debts are a priority. But that isn't the case at all. All of the debt should be treated exactly the same with only two exceptions.

● The first of those exceptions is in the case of a loan being secured by a charge attached to a house or any other property it was used to buy, such as a car or machinery. It is possible to find that charge is enforced and the property returned to the lender if that debt is not properly serviced, although that is highly unlikely if the methods in this programme are followed.

- The second exception is in the case of Court Orders. Usually, they only made in the case of fines or family maintenance payments. Court Orders are not the same as County Court Judgements – they are more important and should be treated as such because the result of ignoring a court order is arrest and being taken before the court in handcuffs and that is an experience best avoided. All of these situations are covered in later chapters.

From the debt list, you need to prioritise the order of repayment, and other information in this book will help you do that. But it is quite possible that several of them, especially the larger ones, can be deferred for a long time. Others can even be written off entirely, either now or at some point in the near future, and this is the best possible outcome. That way the debt is gone forever and you have only had to repay a fraction of it.

Stressful debts

The first thing to do is clear as many stressful debts as possible, at a stroke. Stressful debts are likely to be personal debts to friends and family or to small local shops or the business. Forget the big building societies, banks and credit card companies for the moment – just get rid of all the stressful debts by either paying them at a stroke or agreeing monthly repayments.

Nobody is likely to take court action over debts lower than £200. It costs more than that in time and fees for arranging a hearing. But if anybody refuses your offer of monthly repayment and threatens court action, invite them to go ahead, and to keep you properly informed of any hearing so you may attend and defend yourself. Armed with your financial statement, you will only be ordered to pay whatever it is you originally offered in the first place.

Agreeing very low repayment terms for any debt is very important at this stage. The lower the amount the better, one pound a month is perfect, as will be explained later. Use the standard letters to arrange an agreement and once the letter is sent off, you can forget about the stressful debts. Now we are already making progress.

Debt list

The debt list, or **financial statement** as it will become known, will play a very important role in the road to recovery. To be blunt, if you ever find yourself in a court over any of these debts, a financial statement is the best defence you have. Not only does it demonstrate to the court you are treating the situation seriously, and are on top of it, but it also illustrates quite clearly how much you can afford, if anything, to repay on a monthly basis. But that also means if you are allocating £2,000 per month in restaurant bills or £500 per month on cigarettes, the court is not likely to be very sympathetic and will agree with creditors that their unpaid bill is more important than your social life. Be reasonable with personal expenses and everyone will respect that.

But make sure the budget is prepared heavily in your own favour and do not leave anything out. You must have your priorities in order and if the children need new school uniforms, or the house has to be warm for a new baby, then that is more important than paying off an old clothes account or credit card debt. And most right thinking people agree. The courts certainly agree and the credit agencies and debts collectors know they do. And if you have been sensible, and show you really can only afford to pay a creditor as little as £1 per month, then that is probably all you will end up paying. Don't worry about the interest being greater than that figure each month as you can cover that later and prevent the balance from increasing.

Once the task of listing all the debts is complete you may have ended up owing even more money than you realised. It sometimes happens but it doesn't make any difference. All secured debt is the same and all unsecured debt is the same, regardless of the amount. The hard part is now complete and everything else is easy now you have faced up to the debt and are taking action. If this opening chapter has unnerved you, and you are considering putting the book down, make sure you don't.

You have done the hardest part now and the three golden rules when dealing with a creditor are Contact, Contact and Contact. In one hour from now the letters will be open, the list will be complete and all will be in a file marked Action. The next step is to start contacting everyone you owe money to as the very first step in forgetting debt

From now on you can sleep well again and the postman will not have any more nasty surprises for you in the morning. In fact very soon letters from creditors will be bringing good news.

3. Consolidation loans

Now we are about to begin the task of getting out of debt, on our own terms, but before starting that Positive Action, we ought to have a look at the supposed quick and painless routes out of trouble.

Consolidation loans are rarely a good idea. Why exchange many small unsecured debts that you can negotiate better deals on, for one large inflexible debt that could bankrupt you if you fall behind with the payments again. These loans are widely advertised in all the national newspapers, and increasingly on television, by loan companies ranging from the household names through to some you have never heard of, all offering us a painless way out of debt, by taking on more debt.

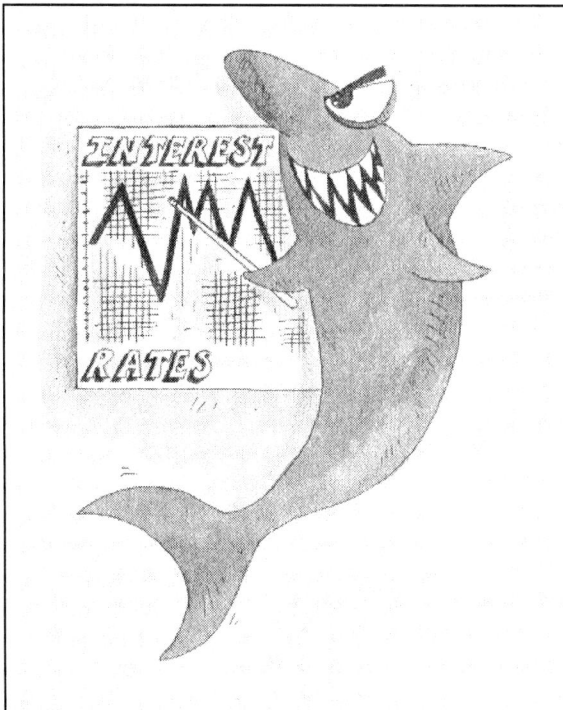

They offer quick decisions and seem at first to be the only way to clear existing problems, but interest rates are high as you are already seen as a bad risk to lenders. Loans with more realistic interest rates are only offered to homeowners, and security for this new loan is required. This means a loan company will require a charge on whatever property you have as security for their loan and that could lead to repossession if you fall behind with the repayments. In effect this means any unforeseen circumstance such as illness or unemployment could lead to the loan company using a charging order to force the sale of your home and recover their money, with interest. It does happen, and it is the reason for much of the repossession we hear about.

Low interest rates versus big risks! Why run those risks just to pay off a few unsecured trivial debts that we can deal with in a much more effective way, or get out of altogether?

It is possible to arrange an unsecured loan with a high street bank or building society and whilst this is a slightly better option, you still become saddled with a larger and less flexible loan than you had before (flexible being the key word) and that cannot be a good thing. The bank could still manage to persuade a court to force the sale of a home or any other asset you have in order to repay the loan. And that is something smaller unsecured creditors will not be able to do.

In a nutshell, having 10 unsecured £1,000 debts puts us in a much stronger position than having one secured £10,000 debt. Small creditors are unable to force us to repay if we are genuinely unable to, and they cannot seize assets without a court order. And a magistrate is unlikely to issue one of those if we are present in court and armed with a financial statement, pleading poverty. Keep creditors apart from each other and don't lump them together. We don't need consolidation loans.

4. Existing debts

Having hopefully decided against that option, the task now is to assess your current financial position, which is probably much stronger than you realise. After all, you have had the money and the only way a lender can get it back effectively is by making it easy for you, not harder. Most unsecured debts are impossible to collect if you genuinely do not have enough money to repay. It doesn't matter about the future and how you might get this or that one job. It's now you are assessing and the reason you have prepared your financial statement is to demonstrate that you genuinely cannot afford to repay it now, not what might happen at a later date. Don't make optimistic predictions about the future, deal only with the present.

At this point you can do one of two things. You can either can let events take their course, which will result in further interest being added until the time of the inevitable county court appearance, followed by court costs. Or you can contact the creditor directly, and as soon as you can, and explain the position you now find ourselves in. A creditor will understand how the court process works and if you show them your financial statement they can also calculate how much a court is likely to award them in monthly repayments should that be the only option. So you need to give them a better option than that.

County court judgments

Believe it or not, there are advantages to a county court judgement and the main one is that as a result of it the debt becomes fixed. No further interest charges will be added, and if you can prove to a Magistrate, by using the Financial Statement, that you can only afford to pay £5 per month, that is all the order is likely to be – however large the debt. The last thing a court will do is force you into the position that leads you to defaulting on the order by insisting you repay more than you can realistically afford.

But the downside here is that a CCJ is registered in your name at your address and from then on it will very difficult to obtain any sort of credit or bank loan in the future, if you list that address. How to overcome that later.

But by pre-empting that process by contacting the creditor early and trying to persuade them they will stand a better chance of your repaying them in full by keeping the courts out of the process, the better chance you have of succeeding. Although – be subtle. You are trying to show your creditor that what you are offering is the maximum you can afford and the best they can hope for, and if they try to get heavy by using the courts, they may end up with even less. The wording of the letter helps this approach.

Another benefit is, if they ignore your attempt to make a suitable arrangement and press ahead with a court action, a magistrate will take a very dim view of their actions. If it is demonstrated that you have tried to resolve the problem properly and directly, a court is likely to try to help you as much as they can. Better still, they may even order the creditor to pay their own costs, instead of adding it to your debt. Creditors know this and try to avoid it.

It is understandable to feel nervous about contacting people you own money to as it is a little like admitting defeat. But don't worry. The creditor will have seen it all before, thousands of times, and are likely to be sympathetic. After all, you have the money, and they are trying to get it back. Who does that put in the strongest position?

This, and other information in this book, will enable you to take advantage of laws, procedures and tricks of the trade, all of which you can use to reduce your debt to an absolute minimum, and to deal with it on your own terms. Whatever happens, and there are always variations in results, we will remove the worry of debt completely. Let's start.

DEAL WITH DEBT
in NINETY MINUTES

Immediate Action
- Starting NOW

2

Immediate Action – Starting NOW

1. Contact your creditors today

You have already opened all those unpaid bills so your financial statement needs to be laid out and easy to understand.

Financial Statement - Mr and Mrs AB Sea

Monthly Net Income   **Expenses**

(what goes into the bank after deductions)

Income		Expenses	
£1150	Salary	£750	Mortgage or Rent
£350	Part time work	£230	Food
£65	BT		
£45	Gas/Elec		
£75	Car/insurance		
£80	Community/Water rates		
£75	Clothing		
£15	School dinners		
£25	Child Care		
£40	Other (everything else)		

Totals

£1500   **£1400**

Net disposable income	£100
Current debt repayments	£350
Shortfall	£250 every month

Now that you know where you stand, you need to write to every creditor you have. But do not include the financial statement until the time you write offering revised repayment terms. At this point you only need to establish exactly what is outstanding, how much it is increasing every month and what interest, if any, is being charged.

Example

Dear Sirs,

RE: Account Number   123 4567-8987-65

Will you please provide me with the following information as soon as possible.

1. A copy of my original credit agreement

2. The total amount outstanding

3. What service charges or interest charges are being added each month

4. The interest rate (if applicable)

5. Is there any unemployment or sickness insurance attached to the agreement? *(This doesn't apply to bills, only loans and credit agreements.)*

I am unable to meet the next two agreed payments and may need to reschedule the repayments altogether. As soon as I hear from you I will be in touch again. *(This buys us a little time and prevents us from worrying about it now we are taking positive action.)*

Yours faithfully,

Insurance

Many companies include unemployment or sickness insurance as a standard part of the agreement. You may be paying for it, but do not necessarily know about it so if those circumstances are the reason for being unable to meet the repayments, then it is worth knowing.

Change of address

If there has been a change of address since the last contact with a particular company, and they do not have the new address, do not give it to them just yet. Use the address they already have and then contact the Post Office and arrange to have all mail sent to there automatically redirected to the new one. It is not expensive and could save a lot of money in the future. If all of our best efforts fail, and the creditor is mean enough to take court action and obtain a judgement, then that judgement may as well be registered at an old address. More about that later.

Review the list

Whilst waiting for replies review the list of debt and with the very next income cheque try to pay off as many of the smaller debts as possible. The fewer we have to think about, even if there is a monthly repayment agreement, the better. For example, if there is a small bank loan with £250 left to pay over the last 6 months, write and ask for the early settlement figure (i.e.; without the last 6 months interest) and then, if possible, pay it off and strike it from your list.

Replies

When the replies start coming in, read them carefully. Especially if they include a copy of the original credit agreement (or application form), read it all including the small print. Now cross-reference it with the chapter Little Known Laws. If a Creditor has breached a law somewhere in any way (and they often do), you will be able to benefit from that at a later date. In reading it through, it may be possible to find there are circumstances where repayment can be deferred, reduced or even insurance claims made that cover those repayments.

Also, keep a record of all replies and the date they were received.

Diary

Devise a diary system, and to those who do not reply within 14 days, send a follow-up letter with a copy of the original. Follow this up again if necessary with a further letter enclosing copies. Keep on top of them, and keep your own copies.

If a reply is still not received within 6 to 8 weeks, put the file away, with copies of all your correspondence and forget about it until later. They can go to the back of the list and by then there may not be any money left over from what is left available to repay all the creditors to offer that particular one much at all, if anything. By then, several amicable repayment schedules may have been agreed and those who have ignored your attempt will find it very difficult to disrupt any of those by insisting on being a priority, whoever they are. They might find themselves agreeing to fifty pence a week.

Time periods

A creditor only has six years in which to recover a debt (three years for marine debts), and they could theoretically remain silent for that long – it does happen. After that, they have no way of recovering a debt and, unless that debt is secured on a property, car or machinery, the slate will be wiped clean. Sometimes even loans secured against the items they were used to purchase, such as a car or business machinery, cannot be repossessed at all. In many cases, property will not be reclaimed if a certain amount of the loan has already been paid off. It may be a third, or half of the agreement, but check the small print. If it is an old loan and several years have already run, then we may find ourselves in a very strong position whereby we can not only reduce the monthly repayment to as low as we can afford, but also to keep the items involved.

The longer a creditor takes to respond, the more likely a court is going to try to assist us. If it can be shown that repeated efforts to sort the problems out with a creditor have been made, the better it is. A creditor refusing to correspond with us, and who continues to charge full interest whilst we are trying to resolve the problems that have arisen, is not going to find a court being very sympathetic towards their position, should it ever get that far.

2. Positive action

Using the financial statement, and the information contained in the replies to the original letter, we can now start to make firm offers in an attempt to reduce the debt, or even eliminate it completely. Look at all the outstanding bills that have no agreed monthly repayment and then decide how much is available. Write offering to repay that bill in monthly instalments, instead of the full amount outstanding.

For example, imagine there is a bill for car repairs, from the local garage, in the sum of £220:

Dear Sirs,

I am writing in relation to my outstanding invoice of £220. My financial situation has changed dramatically over the last few weeks/months and I am not in a position to pay the entire bill at the moment.

I am able to offer monthly payments of £5 over the next 44 months, and I promise to increase these payments as and when I can.

Alternatively I may be able to raise £75 immediately and another £75 next month. Please let me know if this is acceptable to you and we can come to an agreement one way or another over the payment of the invoice.

I look forward to hearing from you.

Yours faithfully,

This is certainly going to get a response and if I was the garage owner, I know what I would do. I would take the £150 and put the rest down to experience. It will cost more than the missing £70 to even consider taking court action. Using this method, coupled with the list of court costs at the end of the book, it is possible to calculate the maximum that should be offered making any legal action against us a waste of time and money.

But if that garage insists on the full amount, then stick to the plan and offer only £5 a month over 44 months. If the money is not available, that is all they will get, even if they do take action in a small claims court. Then, after 6 months of making £5 payments write offering £100 in **full and final settlement**. It is surprising how many will agree to this sort of settlement in order to end the matter and forget all about it.

In practice there are very few who will insist on the full amount. Most will accept something affordable, even if it is a fraction of the amount owed. It is better than nothing and it is quite common for banks and other major lenders to accept as little as 5% in full & final settlement if they are convinced that is all they are going to get. Often they will have insurance against this type of shortfall anyway and can claim it back but to do so they will have to demonstrate they have no chance of receiving the full amount, and they do this by passing on the Financial Statement.

Some of the smaller creditors, especially sole traders or tradesmen, may not be too happy about this. After all, they may be as short of money as the rest of us. However, as long as we are better prepared than they are, there is nothing to worry about. If anybody attempts to 'persuade us' to part with more money than we can afford, refer to the chapter entitled *Harassment*. It is a criminal offence to bully somebody over a debt.

Write to all creditors in the same manner, but for those with agreed monthly repayments such as loan or credit card companies, the letters need to be worded in a different way – asking all of those who charge interest to freeze it, making sure the debt does not get any larger. Some will agree and that is a great start. Those who refuse, pay nothing to – yet. There is no point stretching already tight finances making payments that only just cover interest and service charges, never actually reducing the overall debt. If the worst comes to the worst a debt of £1000, or a debt of £1300 (with the missed payments and added interest) doesn't really make any difference. Not enough to worry about anyway.

Letter to loan or credit card company

Dear Sirs,

RE: account Number   123 - 4567- 89 / 0

I write with regard to the outstanding debt relating to the above account.

Unfortunately I am no longer in a position to meet the monthly payments agreed, and instead propose to repay the balance at a rate of £xx per month. I hope that in 6 months to a year I will be in a position to increase that figure in attempt pay the balance off more quickly.

It will help a great deal if you will freeze the interest so that the debt does not get any larger and I can be in a position to make actual reductions, however small, to the amount owed.

I enclose the card/cheque book etc as I no longer use the facility. As soon as my circumstances change for the better I will inform you immediately. *(Optional but a good idea.)*

I hope this is acceptable to you and I want to confirm I intend paying off this debt in full sooner or later and I hope to able to do it without the courts becoming involved.

Please find enclosed a copy of my current financial statement which outlines my current problem.

Yours faithfully,

This should also get a reply. They may write back asking for more information but the financial statement will have provided most of the information they need. Once they see the position, they are likely to accept any sensible proposal that is presented to them.

If they refuse, the best thing that can happen here is they will quickly take court action. You may be lucky and find the case is thrown out, but as long as you turn up, armed with a copy of the letters outlining the financial position and offering renewed a repayment schedule, the chances are a court will agree that the original offer to the creditor is a reasonable one.

Judgement

The magistrate will set a Judgement against you in the sum of the debt as it stands at that moment. Which means the interest is effectively frozen and the debt cannot get any larger from that point on. That is effectively exactly what we are trying to achieve anyway, so as worst outcomes go, it's not a bad one and the creditor will be left wondering who actually won the court case after all. More of this later in *How to win the Court Case*.

Some people feel that by advising creditors about unemployment or a change in financial circumstances, they will quickly lose confidence in them and apply pressure to have the debt cleared. This is not so. The only time a Creditor will lose confidence is when the problem is ignored or promises to repay at a reduced rate are not kept.

In writing to every creditor like this, however small the concern, we are taking control and are dealing with things positively. From now on, look forward to the postman arriving as he could well be bringing news of an acceptance.

Warning

Failing to keep up re-arranged repayments will look very bad and can work against you should the matter ever end up in court. Creditors, at this early stage, will try to pressurise you into agreeing higher monthly repayments than you have clearly demonstrated are possible. Do not be intimidated, do not be fooled and do not agree to any payment higher than the financial statement shows is available, even if it is only a fraction of the original agreement.

Worried about appearing in court?

The only time to be worried about appearing in court is when you have not kept to the new monthly payments agreed either via that court, or directly with a creditor, so avoid that by only agreeing what is possible. If it is too late, and you have found yourself in that position already, then go back to square one of this book. Start from the beginning, contact all creditors and come clean with everyone about the new financial position. There is nothing wrong with renegotiating.

NB. Do *not* list the names of other creditors on your Financial Statement. You don't have to reveal that at this stage, so don't.

3. Your mortgage/rent – safeguard your home

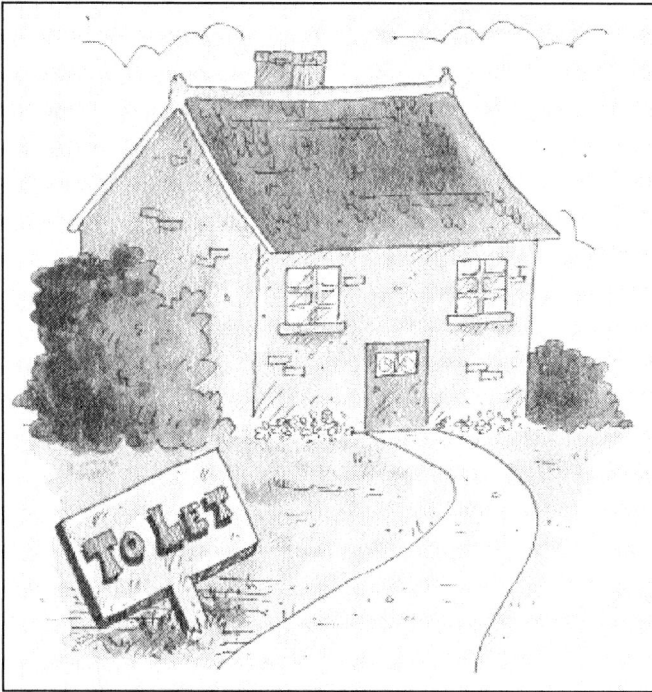

In spite of the current wave of repossessions, there are actually very few mortgage companies in this country who will repossess a family home if it can be avoided in any way at all, and the Government has recently announced measures to ensure that repossession can only be effected as a *last resort*. Naturally lenders will be concerned about the possibility of falling values if there is a risk you may fall into 'negative equity' (i.e. the value of your house is less than the mortgage amount), and more of this later.

However, as long as there is a reasonable margin of value between the mortgage amount and the current value of your property, you are in a good position to negotiate a temporary reduction or suspension of mortgage payments with the lender.

As long as you remain in contact with the lender, and keep them fully informed (which includes providing a copy of the Financial Statement), there is a good chance that they will be both reasonable and flexible. There is no reason at all to lose the family home – especially, as in most cases, other options are always available.

Firstly, all homeowners can make an immediate claim to the Housing Benefit Office to have the monthly interest, or a substantial part of it, paid in the form of housing benefit.

Applicants do not have to be unemployed to claim for housing benefit. The self-employed and those with commission-based income (which is almost any sales role) can also make applications for housing benefit. This means that if there is, or is about to be, a change in circumstances leading to a drop in income, for any reason at all, the HBO is able to make full or part payments by way of benefit, towards mortgage repayments.

Each application is assessed individually and all the HBO need to know is what income has been received over the previous six months, and what is projected over the next six months. In the case of the self-employed, if there is no new work actually booked, then list future income as zero. Commission-based employees should only list the minimum basic salary expected. Don't make predictions of anything higher as it doesn't improve a claim in any way.

Exactly the same benefits are available to tenants living in rented accommodation and exactly the same claim should be made. Start by contacting the Housing Benefit Office and explaining the circumstances, and remember this also applies to those sharing property or renting rooms.

Example

Dear Sirs

I am writing to advise you of a change in my financial circumstance and to enquire which benefits I may be able to claim.

I have been self-employed for over 3 years but over the last 4 months business has been getting slower. I have no new work booked in for the next 4 months but would normally expect to receive at least 3 new contracts during that time in the sum of approximately £3500. With summer approaching, I am expecting my business to be back up and running within 6 months.

Unfortunately this means I now have a period of almost no income at all and would like to know what claims I am able to make in the way of Housing Benefit that will ensure my rent /mortgage repayments over the next 6 months.

Please send out the relevant forms in order for me to make the correct claims.

Many thanks

Yours faithfully

An alternative second paragraph could be:

> My income over the last 3 years has been largely commission based and over the last 4 months our industry has slowed considerably. Have no commission due at all over the next 4 months and will only receive £1500 income during that period. It looks like I may have to start looking for another job but don't want to become unemployed in order to do so.)

Remember – this doesn't automatically mean housing benefit will be awarded, but it's well worth making an application. If there is genuine hardship, the HBO will usually provide some support which in turn leaves one thing less to worry about.

Quite often the HBO will offer to pay your landlord or mortgage lender direct but as there is usually a delay in processing applications, lenders and landlords will need to be kept properly informed. There is no point leaving the HBO to deal with the payment and forgetting about because, if an application is delayed past the monthly payment date, it is you who will receive the nasty letters and telephone calls, not them. Which is exactly what we are working to avoid, so make sure everyone who needs to know, does know.

Example

Dear Sirs

RE: account number 123-4567-890

I am writing to let you know my financial circumstances have unfortunately taken a turn for the worse.

I have applied to the housing benefit office for assistance with my loan/rent repayments and you should be hearing from them in due course. In the meantime, there may be a delay leading to a payment being made, but I am assured all claims are backdated.

Please let me know when the housing benefit office has been in contact.

Yours faithfully

NB: Modify this letter to suit individual circumstances.

Of course, there will be a variety of reasons whereby a landlord or lender cannot be informed of a change in financial circumstances, and in those cases make sure it is made clear to the HBO that no direct contact should be made.

It will be a huge relief to know the rent or mortgage is going to be covered over a few difficult months, allowing time to make alternative long-term arrangements. At the same time and with the same application, assistance will be arranged in respect of council tax charges. Relief will be applied, reducing the amount payable considerably.

Missing mortgage payments

Before the Credit Crunch, it was quite possible to miss a few months mortgage repayments without a lender becoming too heavy-handed. In the current economic climate, it is advisable to inform the lender of your situation BEFORE you miss a payment. However, provided you keep the lender informed of your situation, it is unlikely that one or two missed payments will provoke too extreme a reaction. In fact a lender will usually suggest or even encourage a reduced monthly rate for a short period until a borrower can make other long-term arrangements. Then, at the end of the year, unpaid and outstanding amounts are simply added to the overall loan, spreading it out over future payments.

This is called *capitalising the arrears*. If there are already arrears, ask your lender about this.

If it is too late for that, and the repossession process has already started, don't worry about it but act NOW. The process can easily be stopped right up until the last minute. Send the letter with a copy of your financial statement to your lender, and copy in the local branch, the Housing Benefit Office and, if applicable, the court including the case number at the top. Make sure everyone knows you have taken the first steps to resolve the problem. Where rented property is concerned, do exactly the same thing to your landlord, their solicitor, the HBO and the court.

Rented accommodation

In **rented accommodation** is much easier to be evicted for non-payment than it is by a mortgage lender. The first rule here is to keep your landlord informed. Many of them, especially private landlords, rely on your rent to supplement their own income, and if it isn't paid in on time, their own payments might start bouncing back through lack of funds in their account. And they are not going to be pleased about that.

Whatever the circumstances are, make an immediate application for housing benefit with the local council. You can apply for housing benefit even if you are in work, especially self-employed or running a small business. No matter what your turnover is, if you aren't making enough money to live on, you can claim housing benefit, and you don't need to queue up every two weeks to sign on as it is not unemployment benefit. All they ask for is your financial statement covering the previous six months showing very low income and they will award you benefit calculated on those figures. The lower your profits or income, the higher your housing benefit. And it is reviewed every six months which provides you with plenty of breathing space.

If you have children, but they only stay with you at weekends – as is common in many households these days – you still qualify as you need to provide room for them. A key tip here is to keep the child benefit book in any separation agreement. If you have this in *your* name, your likely benefit income will rise dramatically. Don't make the mistake of handing over child benefit as part of a separation agreement unless you have to, as it could make a big difference in the long run.

In the letter to the landlord, ask for a little time so sort your financial affairs out, and offer to make a reduced payment for a few months until your benefit claims are assessed. Usually they are done in a matter of weeks but it is better to be pessimistic here and not too optimistic.

Example

Dear Mrs Landlord

RE: 123 Any Street

I am writing to let you know my financial circumstances have unfortunately taken a turn for the worse.

I have applied to the housing benefit office for assistance with my rent payments and I expect to hear from them within a few weeks. In the meantime, I know I am going to be unable to meet this month's rent payment in full, although I am able to pay £400 this month and £400 the following month. This will leave a shortfall of £300 per month but I hope to be in a position to repay that by the end of the fourth month when my affairs are straight again.

I have included your name and address on the application form so you may hear from the housing benefit office directly. Please let me know if you do.

I am hoping this is only a temporary situation and will keep you informed.

Yours sincerely

I do not believe there is any court in the land who will grant a possession order in these circumstances and even if you find yourself taken to court six months later, if you can point to correspondence like this on your file, it is highly unlikely you will find yourself on the wrong end of a judgement.

However, it is also worth noting that a landlord is able to apply for a possession order under the terms of an Assured Shorthold Tenancy Act (the most common form of tenancy) at any time after the initial six-month period, with only two months' notice. If you have contacted them in the manner set out here, and kept them fully informed of your situation, and the first thing they do is apply to a court for a possession order, which some do to protect their own interests, then make sure you, in turn, look after your own affairs first. Don't pay any more than you can afford and save the money instead, as you may need that for a deposit on another property in a few months' time.

Eviction

If you end up being evicted, the Council will regard you as *intentionally homeless* and will not offer you council accommodation. You will need to have enough saved for a deposit and the first month's rent on alternative, privately rented accommodation. Follow these simple principles and you can sleep soundly knowing your family will not be out on the street in the coming months. Remember, a landlord ultimately has the law on his side, but it doesn't mean you are without options. Possession really is nine tenths of the Law, so just for good measure, change the locks in case your landlord has a spare set of keys. It has been known for some people to arrive home and find they can't get in. It's illegal of course, but try finding someone interested in helping you at 9pm on a cold winter's night, when you are locked out.

If your landlord is not going to be reasonable with you, then move to another property and then include the old landlord in with your other creditors. Let him fight it out with the professionals you also owe money to. Landlords very rarely pursue unpaid rents. Besides, if you are going to use the Post Office mail redirection service, then they don't need to know your new address.

4. Household services

The Gas, Electricity and Water companies will not deprive you of any services, even as a last resort, if you are in touch with them. They might threaten to, and phone you up at all hours under the masquerade of it being the 'only time most of our customers are at home.' They send you messages via the Post Office's electronic messaging service saying nothing, but giving you an urgent number to ring.

If they do that, *don't phone it*, send it back with the following note:

Dear Sirs

RE: The enclosed letter

I would like to know, by return mail please, what this is, whom it is from and what it refers to. I would also like to know who at BT allows this sort of anonymous harassment and intimidation. I intend to initiate your full complaint procedure and ask you never to send this sort of threatening mail to me again. I look forward to hearing what I have to do to begin this complaint.

Everyone knows where to find me and these people, whoever they are, can either telephone or write to me in the proper manner.

Please do not ignore this as, if you fail to inform me what this is all about, I shall make formal complaints against your firm and theirs, and obtain a restraining order preventing you from harassing me like this again

Yours faithfully

That should stop them, shouldn't it. No more anonymous threatening letters from them.

You may also encounter problems at junior clerk level in some of these national companies from those keen to make an impression and get on in life. Some feel it their duty to impose their authority on those of us who have landed upon hard times, and they will run and hide behind the rules.

Fact: Regardless of their rules and company policy, they have laws to abide by (see little known laws).

If representatives from utility firms phone you at 9pm in the evening or on a Sunday afternoon, politely ask for the name of who you are speaking to.

NB – this is very important, as they will all deny being the one who spoke to anyone who complains. Once you have the caller's name, he or she will follow the rules to the letter. Then ask the caller to make the following note on their file. '(Utility Company Ltd) … is not to make any calls to this number again making demands for money at any time, especially after 6pm and at weekends.' Also explain to them you have written to their customer services department with a proposal to try to resolve the problem. They won't phone again during unsociable hours.

Once again, using the financial statement, write in and explain to each of the utility companies your current or expected future position. It is much better to warn them in advance but if it is too late and there is already an unpaid bill which is causing anxiety, then pay part of it. Take photocopies of the bill, in order to have several copies of the payment giro slip at the bottom with your account details printed on it, and use those to make regular payments of as much as you can as often as you can. This is particularly a good idea after the heavy winter months because within 4 to 6 months not only will the debt be considerable reduced, but the new bills will be considerably lower, easing the overall debt problem.

Most utility companies refuse to allow customers to switch over to a monthly direct debit repayment scheme until any outstanding bill is paid off in full. This is particularly unhelpful but easily overcome by copying the giro slips and making monthly payments that way. As long as a customer is communicating with a utility company, and making regular payments, a court will not issue a warrant of disconnection.

Rights of access

Which leads to their rights of access. To enter a property, a domestic services provider will require a warrant issued by a court. To obtain this warrant, there must be a hearing to which you should be invited. A summons, they call it, but it really is only an invite. You have done nothing wrong in getting behind on your gas or electricity bill. Accept their invitation, turn up with your financial statement and details of the payments you have made and explain to the magistrate the temporary financial problem. He or she will be more sympathetic than expected and they do not talk down or criticise defendants. In fact, the chances are they will be on your side. Hard as that is to believe, they really are.

This means that if the meters are inside the house, no one can enter the property to disconnect. If they are outside, then make sure the meter cupboard has a padlock on it. To disconnect vital services, they need a warrant unless they have external access to your meter and the only way they can get a warrant is by convincing a court you have made no attempt to contact them and resolve the problem. They may decide you have moved out, and to leave services connected to the property may endanger neighbours, in which case a warrant of entry will be issued.

If you have a fear of courtrooms, and many of us do, write a letter instead, explaining the circumstances and why you couldn't attend the court hearing. Enclose the financial statement along with an offer of payment of whatever is affordable by way of a fixed agreement. Supplement that by offering to increase that payment in the coming months, as and when your circumstances improve as a means of clearing the arrears.

It is likely a magistrate will accept that, rather than go to all the expense of rescheduling the hearing. But if you attend court in person it always improves your chances of a settlement which you will find manageable.

Here is a true story. Mr J was paying his electricity account monthly by standing order. He was unemployed and had a young family, including a 3-month old baby, and his house was all electric. They relied upon electricity totally. His winter bill came through, and as he had a padlock on the meter cupboard, found it was based on an estimation. It turned out to be over-estimated by £100 but he thought nothing of it, expecting things to even themselves out, confident that he was paying the correct amount. He continued to pay the same but very quickly – in fact within a single month – the electricity company sent him a demand for his 'shortfall'. He ignored it, so they sent him a disconnection notice. He tried then to reason with them, but after holding in a telephone queue listening to 80s pop ballads for 45 mins, he gave up. He knew they would need a warrant so he would have to be informed of a court hearing, at which he felt he could easily demonstrate the over-estimation, and probably even claim his costs back.

Within a month, somebody turned up with an official-looking clip board implying he had a warrant to disconnect the service. Mr J asked him to think carefully about what he was saying because he couldn't have a warrant without a court hearing, and Mr J would have known about that. Mr J suggested that if the man was telling lies in order to gain entry to his house, he would call the Police and an immediate change of tone followed. Man with clipboard became a little less threatening.

A final tip is to check all domestic service bills, especially those that have been estimated. Have the meter read as usually bills are over-estimated and it is quite possible that any outstanding bills are higher than they really should be. These may be debts that can be reduced or even struck off completely.

Council Tax

Finally, we come to the Council Tax. Tempting as it is, don't ignore this department. It's interesting that of all the people you will have to deal with, this lot appear to be the most unhelpful. That doesn't mean all of them, but 90% are badly trained and badly paid, which means only the unskilled apply for these sorts of jobs. Consequently lots of mistakes are made, but they are also the one of the few creditors who can obtain an actual arrest warrant for non-payment, so don't ignore them.

All low income families, and families with no income at all, qualify for Council Tax Benefit and many can claim either full or part assistance they were not even aware of. If an application has been made for housing benefit, then an automatic assessment will also be made for Council Tax Benefit and outstanding bills are either credited or adjusted. If you haven't applied then make sure you do as it's one thing less to worry about. But either way, once again write in explaining the circumstances enclosing the Financial Statement. You will find that department generally accepts any proposal you make to clear the arrears monthly. It doesn't usually matter how low the payment, as long as it is something and it is regular.

Help desks

All benefit offices have help desks. Ask somebody to explain all the benefits available – it is usually more than you think.

5. Credit cards

For many years, credits cards have been freely available to almost anybody, with absurdly high spending limits. After the Credit Crunch that all changed of course, but this is no consolation for people already in the clutches of credit card lenders.

Just about every major lender offered a credit card facility and the reason for this was because they made so much money out of them through the extrortionate interest rates charged. Now they are trying to reduce their exposure, and this is bringing an unwelcome squeeze to many people who find themselves needing to repay or reduce their credit card borrowings.

Credit cards have traditionally offered a tempting access to on-tap borrowings (unlike debit cards which take payments directly from an account with funds in). They started off as interest-free arrangements and it is not surprising they were so attractive (and remain attractive to those who are still able to utilise this source of funds). Some people use the loan facility during the interest free initial period and then apply for a new interest free card from another source and transfer the balance, repeating this as often as possible, effectively extending the period of the interest free loan. Some people have more than one card and borrow from one to pay another, every month.

This is a way of transferring balances around but there is always only one result. Eventually interest payments will be charged and this becomes one of the most expensive ways of borrowing money. When it becomes clear that repayments are difficult or even impossible to afford, consolidation loans are offered, usually secured against a property or other assets, and that is when the trouble starts. Credit card facilities are essentially unsecured loans and this means once borrowers have found themselves unable to meet repayment schedules, a credit card company will find it very difficult, if not impossible, to get their money back. This is why options to consolidate these loans are always secured against property.

Write to these companies in the manner outlined in the *Positive Action* chapter and all credit card worries will evaporate. They know that unsecured loans are hard, if not impossible, to recover and will usually do all they can to help you out. But *do not consider any form of consolidation loan* in these cases. There is no point at all in turning several unsecured credit card debts into one large secured debt, usually secured against your property. This doesn't resolve any financial problems, it makes them worse.

6. Car/equipment loans

The same principle applies to car loans or other equipment loans although there is one major difference. Usually these are secured against the item the loan is used to purchase, and in this case a loan company is entitled to ask for that item back. But they all differ and, in many cases, loan companies are not able to reclaim the item if a certain percentage of the loan has already been repaid. Check the small print of the loan or hire purchase agreement. It could be 25%, it could be 33% or even as much as half of the loan, but the fact is if you have already reached a certain point with the repayment schedule of any agreement then you are entitled to keep the item the loan was used to buy.

In such a case, write to the finance company, enclosing a copy of your Financial Statement, and offer a revised repayment schedule of whatever you have demonstrated you can afford, even if it is only a fraction of the originally agreed amount. But make sure the interest rate is frozen as there is no point making monthly repayments only to find the amount outstanding continues to increase. If a finance company refuses, then pay nothing. Any court action they take will result in a judgement that will freeze the interest rate and you will not be ordered to pay more than you can reasonably afford on a monthly basis.

Then, in a year's time, write offering a full and final payment, even if this is only a small percentage of the outstanding amount, by way of settlement. It is surprising how many finance companies will agree to such arrangements in order to clear a debt from their book.

7. Student loans

One of the most highly publicised forms of debt is the Student Loan Scheme. It basically means that all university undergraduates who are unable to afford to pay their own tuition fees can apply for an interest-free loan from the Department of Education and Employment, via the Student Loan Company Ltd. There are various loan schemes covering full- or part-time education as well as loans for accommodation and living expenses, and, in some cases, hardship loans. Each application differs depending upon student circumstances, the nature of the course and university or college attended (as their course fees differ). One thing remains consistent for everybody and that is a build up of debt by the time of graduation.

All loans have to be repaid, including those where students have failed to complete their course for any reason and it is virtually unavoidable, although there are some ways round it for some people.

The idea that a student might just change address or vanish into the system is a non-starter as all loan schemes are attached to an individual's national insurance number and subsequent Tax Code. As soon as that person starts earning above a pre-set amount, whether they have finished their courses or not (although this doesn't

includes summer time work and gap years) the Tax Office is obliged to make scaled deductions directly from any income in order to start making repayments to the Student Loan Company.

The average debt a student incurs during the term of his or her higher education is around £18,000. It is a lot of money by anybody's standards but graduates are only obliged to start paying any of it back once they reach a minimum earning level, which is the same for everybody – presently £15,000.

The easy solution is to simply forget all about it, as it doesn't really affect anybody. A graduate starting out on her working career might as well do so without even thinking about being saddled with debt as repayments are deducted at source along with Tax and National Insurance contributions, which we all have to make. In this case, it simply becomes a cost of living and it is regarded as such, not a debt.

And not a very large one at that. A graduate starting work on £20,000 per year will end up paying under £9 a week off on the student loan, which is about 3 Bacardi Breezers and a kebab in student currency. This is known as income-contingent repayments and it comes into effect after graduation from the course the loan relates to, even if a graduate goes on to enrol in a further course.

Income threshold will vary, and increase in line with inflation but the principle will remain the same. Once graduates start receiving income above a certain level, Student Loan Repayments will start to be deducted from their salary. In the case of the self-employed, repayments will become due under the self-assessment scheme and will be included in any Income Tax bill or assessment.

There are some key points to remember;

1. Any income of a husband, wife, partner, parent or any other relative will not be taken into account

2. Any income received via Child Benefit or Disability Benefit does not get taken into account.

3. Any graduate who makes payments via employer deduction will also have to make payments via the self-assessment scheme if they are required to submit one (in the case of an employee also carrying out part time work).

4. Graduates working abroad and outside the UK Tax system are obliged to inform the SLC of any income. The SLC will then calculate repayments on the same basis as UK taxpayers and make arrangements to collect them with a graduate directly.

5. Extra repayments can be made at anytime and in any way a graduate chooses, and they will be deducted from the total amount outstanding.

If a graduate is a non-UK taxpayer and fails to inform the SLC of any income there may be penalties. These are;

1. The SLC can triple the normal rate of interest on any account if a graduate fails to
    *   advise the SLC of living overseas (regardless of any earnings)
    *   provide the SLC any information they ask for in respect of overseas status.

2. The SLC can base repayments on an income of TWICE the UK national average if a graduate fails to provide full information of oversees earnings.

3. The SLC reserves to right to accelerate the debt if repayments are continually missed – which means a court order can be obtained to recover the full amount in one payment.

Refunds

If during the course of a year, a graduate only works for part of that year, but deductions have been made, then it is possible to apply to the SLC for a refund if the total earnings will average out at less than the minimum amount. For example, if a graduate works for four months on a £24,000 a year contract then deductions will be made from the beginning. If that graduate ceased to work having only earned £8,000 for that year, then a refund is due on all repayments deducted at source. Refunds have to be applied for and will not be considered automatically.

However there are some ways around repaying a student loan, and these are as follows.

Not ideal ways:

1. a graduate reaches the age of 65
2. a graduate dies before the loan is fully repaid (meaning beneficiaries of an estate are not liable)
3. a graduate becomes permanently disabled.

The ideal ways:

Many major employers now, including some Government Departments, are competing for high achieving graduates to work for their companies. So much so that some of the world's largest companies are wining, dining and generally courting careers advisors at universities across the country in an attempt to persuade them to recommend graduates to their organisation. This has become so competitive that many employers are offering graduates 'Golden Hellos' in an attempt to secure their services in favour of a rival employer. Golden Hello's include offers to repay directly any student loans, either in one lump sum or spread out over an initial training period. This is a major incentive for any graduate, not only being offered an agreeable package, but the chance to have their entire student loan paid of in one go.

Naturally there are penalties and claw backs due if a graduate stops working for that particular employee prior to the completion of the initial agreed period, but these all differ and are subject to negotiation. The best place to find out about employers who offer such a scheme is through the University Careers Board. Each board is in regular touch with employers and many incentives are available to high achieving graduates, which they should be aware of.

This doesn't mean a graduate shouldn't consider raising this issue with any employer when negotiating the terms of an employment contract. If an employer is keen to make use of your education, then there is no harm in asking them to contribute towards it. But the actual repayment schedules are deliberately small enough to enable former students to comfortably be able to repay their student debt.

Some people argue that university education should be free, enabling graduates to embark on their careers free of debt as they are more likely to become high achievers and therefore high earners in later life. The theory being that their correspondingly increased level of taxation should repay the investment made in their university education. But that is like suggesting footballers, who can earn vast sums of money, should have all their early coaching and equipment free, or that musicians who can earn large taxable incomes one day should have all their equipment, travel and lessons paid for by the government. Or perhaps that writers should be paid to write their books by the State. The truth is that we have to understand that we can't always expect other people to invest in our own futures, and that we are all responsible ourselves for that.

More information about student loans can be found at the student support website **www.dfes.gov.uk/studentsupport** or at the Student Loans Company website **www.slc.co.uk** or by telephoning 0800 405010. Check regularly as the regulations are changing all the time.

A complete guide handbook can be downloaded at **www.dfes.gov. uk/studentsupport/formsandguides.cfm**

8. Child Support Agency

The Child Support Agency was established in 1995 to save taxpayers money by off-setting the benefit costs of parents against an absent parent's income, although it often reported that its own costs are running so high that it fails to do that. In fact the cost to the Agency for every £100 recovered is only £25.98, apparently proving its worth.

During the writing of this book, the laws and the CSA's own systems and procedures changed several times and this section became out of date twice during the writing process alone. Therefore it is safer to refer back to the section explaining the Financial Statement, which will as always prove to be useful, and recommend the following websites for up-to-date, accurate information:

http://www.childsupportadvice.co.uk

www.csa.gov.uk

http://www.ondivorce.co.uk/childsm.htm

DEAL WITH DEBT
in NINETY MINUTES

Income

3

Income

1. The DSS

Should you be unemployed, or in a low paid job that doesn't cover your monthly outgoings properly, then it is important to make full use of the laws and regulations and benefits available. It is not only the unemployed who are entitled to claim benefits. Any person genuinely struggling to make ends meet should contact the Benefits Agency immediately as there is a wide range of assistance available covering a variety of circumstances. But, by the time you do so, it is important to have agreements in place with as many of your creditors as possible.

The first step is to write to the local Benefits Agency, enclosing your Financial Statement and ask for advice and application forms for whatever benefit is available to you. The Agency will know exactly what you can and cannot claim for and will send out the relevant application forms.

Grants

Also ask about grants. Many are available for the installation of heating or insulation, especially during the winter months, for low income families. When applying for a grant, ask for information on how the applications are assessed and what does or doesn't qualify. You may find the limit for grants are perhaps £1,000 and if you apply for £1,050, it will be automatically rejected, without your being informed why. If you have that information in the first place, you have a better chance of succeeding with an application.

There are all sorts of grants available from the social fund. Find out what you can apply for – you may be surprised. If you are turned down ask why. You can re-apply or appeal and the Social Fund inspector will review your application. DSS staff are generally helpful but the general attitude is to 'play thing by the book'. This means something in an application might prevent a person claiming one sort of benefit or grant, leading to a rejection. But there may be an alternative that the same person could qualify for so, each time you have an application turned down, ask for an alternative.

Set aside a day to read through all DSS literature and send in applications for everything possible and ask about anything you are not sure about. There are help lines that cover most enquiries and all Benefits Agencies have a help desk.

Example

> Mr J applied for a grant to have the electric storage heaters replaced in his otherwise unheated house. He was unaware that the limit for a grant of this nature was £1,000, as nobody at the Benefits Agency had bothered to tell him this when the application forms were sent out. As a result, he submitted a claim for £1050, which took the Agency three months to reject on the grounds that it exceeded the fund's limit for an individual application. When he was told the reason Mr J simply reapplied claiming £1,000 for exactly the same heaters, and the grant was awarded. Unfortunately four months had passed by and the winter was over.

Benefits for the low paid and unemployed also stretch to food and milk payments (especially if you have young children) and free dental and eye care and medical prescriptions. Make it your business to collect all the literature and leaflets explaining the entire range of benefits and grants available. To properly cover the complete benefit section in this chapter is not possible, especially as the options vary and change on a regular basis. Contact your local Benefits Agency and explain the situation fully and ask for information about what assistance is available. Contact them via their website, or on the telephone numbers listed in your local directory.

The Benefits Agency Website can be found at – **http://www.dwp. gov.uk.**

2. Pooling your income

Using your budget, you should lump all income in together, wherever it comes from. It could be a combination of salary and income support, child benefit and part time wages.

Whatever it is – pool it together. It could be that if children are old enough to contribute, they can do just that. Any pocket money children earn is usually wisely spent, but money they are given is often wasted and we cannot be too young to learn the lesson of debt and keeping clear of it. A family, as a unit, needs to work together in order to get out of debt. The burden of that problem should be shared, but it must be done sensitively.

Once you have worked out the family fund, allocate a sum to each item on your list of expenses. Some people, especially those who receive all of their income in cash, use envelopes (or jars) to save for each different household expense. Referring to their budget, they will divide cash up and place the allocated amount in its relevant envelope.

Many people use this system effectively, although there are disadvantages.

1. You will need to take a trip into town, or to the nearest post office, in order to pay all the bills every month.

2. You will be tempted to borrow from one fund to make up a short fall in another, Don't...! If you haven't got enough for the electricity people, then write and tell them. Don't cause problems with another fund instead.

3. Using this method is insecure. Don't leave a jar on the kitchen shelf stuffed with cash marked 'Rent Money'.

3. Protecting your income

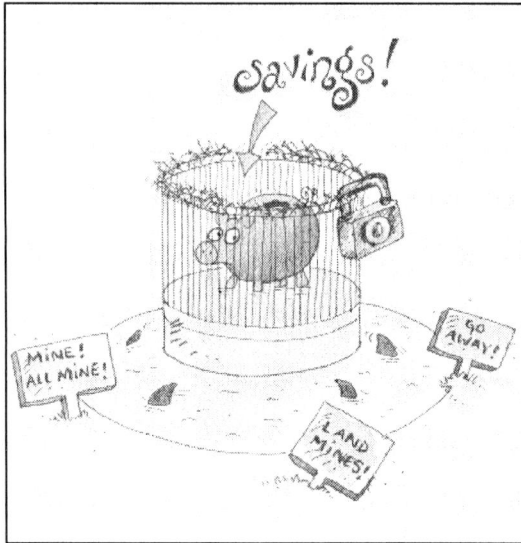

The only two effective ways a creditor can get at your income before you do are by way of a 'garnishee order' or an 'attachment of earnings order', as described below.

Garnishee Order

If a court finds in favour of your creditor (which they always will if you do actually owe the money), then they give you opportunities to come up with a repayment scheme. Failing to attend court or reply to any of the correspondence they issue will lead to, as a last resort, the court imposing a Garnishee Order which instructs a bank or employer to pay the money owed, directly to your creditor without any reference to you. In effect, an employer may be forced to pay an employee's wages directly to a creditor instead.

Attachment of Earnings Order

In the case of larger debt, where the money in an account or wage packet doesn't cover the debt in one lump sum, then a creditor can apply to the court for an **Attachment of Earnings Order**. If granted, the court will order an employer to make a monthly deduction from a salary. This is then paid directly into the court who will, in turn, pass it onto a creditor.

Of course, in this extreme case, you will wish you had never told anybody where you work and who your employer is because without that knowledge, attachment to earnings orders are almost impossible to grant. The same applies for garnishee orders. If your creditor or the court doesn't know who you bank with, then they cannot issue such an order. So beware who you give your bank details to, and more importantly, who you write cheques out to. Some creditors photocopy cheques before paying them in simply to keep that sort of information on their file, which may be useful to them in the future.

But it is unlikely any action will ever get that far. It certainly never needs to if the principles in this book have been adopted. In most cases, attending a court with a Financial Statement is enough to persuade a magistrate that you are taking the debt seriously and making an attempt to resolve the problem. In these cases, a magistrate is unlikely to do anything that makes it worse and that includes garnishee orders and attachment to earnings orders, especially if such an order may have an adverse effect on a person's relationship with his or her employer.

Protected earnings level

At this stage, ask the Court registrar to set a 'protected earnings level'. This will be a sum of money you must have every month to pay for essential items which are the priorities on the Financial Statement. The court will also take into consideration any repayments amicably agreed out of court with other creditors. It is unlikely a court will give your creditor, who has ignored your previous attempts to agree a realistic repayment scheme, any priority over creditors who have already accepted your proposals.

As a final request, you can ask a court to give you the opportunity to make voluntary payments, which they should agree to and this will prevent your employer knowing of your difficulties. But this means your creditor can re-approach the court any time they like if you fail to keep up those payments. You might as well get it out of the way now and accept the court ruling, especially as it will probably be in your favour. If however, the court does decide to grant the attachment to earnings order, you still have an ace up your sleeve. You will be asked to fill in a Form N 56. At the bottom of this form a question asks how much you are prepared to have deducted from your salary. Only fill in the amount you have previously offered. Don't conceded defeat at this late stage. If you have only offered £5 previously, stick to that offer.

The real beauty of this sort of agreement is that once the court has set the repayments levels, however low, then that's it. It won't change. You may then find yourself in a position to approach that creditor at a later date and make an offer in full and final settlement of a much lower figure than the remaining outstanding debt. Most companies take the view that accepting a reasonable final payment will be better that continuing to receive £5 per month for the next 30 years. Your creditor may think they are being clever in taking you to court, but they are the only ones who can lose here and they know that. That is why professional companies nearly always agree vastly reduced repayments proposals without involving the courts once they have seen your financial statement and understand your financial position.

4. Limiting your outgoings

Working with your budget, you can make cut-backs that will allow a little extra money for emergencies, or even luxuries – extra money that your creditors need never know about. They are small cut-backs which when lumped together form their own fund.

For a start, always try to stay 10% inside your budget. If your food fund is £60 per week, try to find a way of getting that down to £54, every week. Finding a cheaper shop or using cheaper products is actually an easy thing to do. Turn the heating down a few notches and use expensive electrical items like washing machines, tumble dryers – or even cook meals overnight – on the cheaper electricity rate. It sounds petty, but you can easily save as much as £1 per day on electricity, or £30 per month. It is estimated that in Britain alone we waste £300 million every month through apathy and ignorance.

5. Money you didn't know you had

Keep a track of money, and don't rely on others to do that for you as it can disappear at an alarming rate if you do. There are thousands of examples of major banks or building societies who debit accounts twice every month for the same payment. They don't necessarily know it is a mistake and it is up to the customer, you, to check statements every month. This can lead to rapidly growing debt and increasing bank charges. Left unchecked for four months, this can cause embarrassment and significant overdraft fees, which could easily have been avoided by checking the statements and making a simple phone call. Even if the problem is not noticed for several months, a bank will always refund the overpayment and bank charges once the mistake is identified, but they won't identify it for you. Don't leave statements unopened in the back of a drawer – check them for yourself.

Another example saw a creditor continuing to take payments from a customer's account, which was agreed by a court, for four months after the agreement was paid off in full. It is possible that particular creditor did it simply to be awkward, and even major companies can be this small minded, if they employ small-minded people. But it is also possible they made a policy of continuing to take repayments after the agreement with the court has been completed. Don't let this happen to you.

Keep an eye on things and cancel agreements at least two months before the final repayment is due. This is mainly because some systems take over 28 days to effect a cancellation but it also leaves you in a stronger position as, at the end of the agreement, it is you who owes them money, not the other way round. Let them write to you and ask for the final payment by cheque. If they forget to, then that's their problem. You could always remind them. But it's money you didn't know you had.

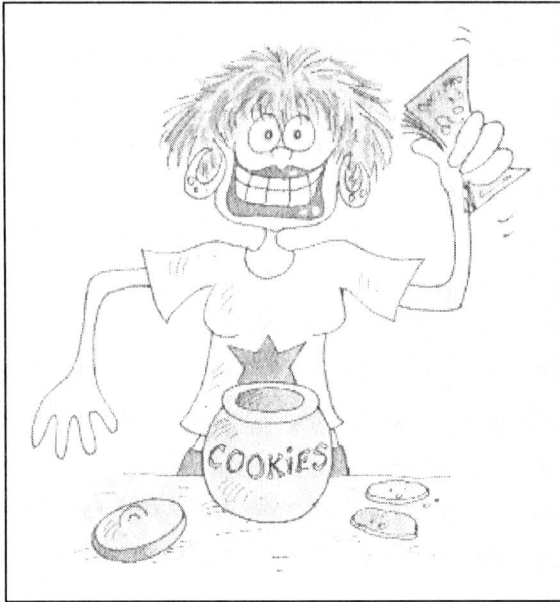

Write to the Inland Revenue. They regularly overcharge people tax and it is up to us to ask for it back. If your income has dropped suddenly, or ceases altogether, you may find they had been charging you tax on an estimate of your next two years earnings, based on the previous two years. If that has changed, the Inland Revenue may well owe you money. Ask for a review and a rebate. One lady, who had been made redundant from a high salaried position, found she was due over £2,800 in rebates, payable immediately, simply by explaining her new financial position to the Inland Revenue and asking for a review.

Ask everybody you make payments to check their records for over payments. It could be your mortgage company has been setting your monthly repayments using an old, higher interest rate than they should have been, and you may be due a repayment or reduction in future repayments. Ask for a statement of your account and make sure the tax relief on the mortgage loan is set at the correct rate. One man found he had never received tax relief on his mortgage and was due five years of £80 a month back. That's £4,800. Ask for interest to be added to that repayment as they are quick to charge it when an account is in arrears.

If you have become unemployed or unfit to work, check every creditor you have for unemployment or sickness insurance. Many loans, credit agreements and mortgages have this sort of insurance built in to the loan agreement, which you may have been paying for without realising it. Some home and health insurance policies also have sickness and unemployment clauses so it is worth enquiring with everybody you make a monthly payment to, whatever it is.

Finally, get rid of all that junk in the loft or garage. Sell the lot of it and use that money to pay off all the small niggling debts in one hit. One or two car boot sales could pay off a number of small worrying personal debts, at a stroke.

6. Tax Credits

Working Tax Credit and Child Tax Credits are part of a Government initiative for assisting low-income individuals and families. Tax Credits are available from April 2003 to anyone over 16 years of age normally living in the United Kingdom, including married or unmarried couples, who are in paid employment for at least sixteen hours per week and to anybody over 25 years of age if they are in paid employment for at least 30 hours a week. This includes single parents, the disabled and the self-employed, either in partnership or sole trading. The idea is to improve the income of the low paid by enabling them to find work without running the risk of losing all their benefits, but it also works in favour of those in part-time work or for the self-employed who are struggling to make ends meet.

Full up to date details of the Tax Credit system can be found at the Inland Revenue's website: **http://www.taxcredits.inlandrevenue. gov.uk** where applicants can complete an online assessment form to find out which tax Credits are available.

DEAL WITH DEBT
in NINETY MINUTES

The Law

4

The Law

1. Repossession – voluntary or otherwise

Many people are terrified of their building societies and banks, and feel that even if their manager so much as suspects a borrower is out of work, and possibly unable to meet their monthly repayments, their home will be at risk.

It is a common mistake, but one that leads people to shy away from dealing with potential problems early enough for them to be avoided. The first thing to do, preferably before any payments are missed, is to contact the mortgage lender. Most, if not all mortgage lenders are quick to re-schedule payments if they are made aware in advance of a financial problem that may lead to any missed payments, either in the short or long term.

It is quite possible to have several mortgage repayments reduced to an affordable amount, even to nothing at all for a few months, if there is a good reason for it. Although this results an arrears on the account at the end of the year, they will show on your overall statement, and future payment levels can be set to allow for this. For example, if your mortgage is £80,000, and you fail to make six payments in a year (with agreement), then your end-of-year statement might show the outstanding mortgage loan balance as £82,000 (assuming interest at 5.0%). It is then possible to ask your lender to calculate all future payments on that figure, meaning your mortgage is now £82,600 instead of £80,000. This results in the six missing payments being spread over the remaining term of your mortgage. It is called *Capitalisation of Arrears* and it will see you through a difficult year without worrying about the debt that is accruing or having property repossessed.

Debt on a lender's branch books is bad for branch managers but if they have made provision for it in advance, by being properly informed, it will reflect well on the manager and that will be good for you. Whenever the housing market is flat, and people find the value of their homes less than the mortgage on it, some choose to 'hand back the keys'. Often, when the mortgage is many thousands of pounds higher than the value of the property, it is understandable.

Don't forget other debts may well also be accruing and with them listed against a current present address, some people find moving on may be a good idea for a number of reasons.

But voluntary repossession doesn't absolve a borrower of the responsibility of the mortgage interest payments right up until the time the house is sold by the building society. Nor can you avoid still being responsible for the shortfall, should the house be sold for less than the mortgage and the costs of selling it.

If a borrower is thinking of walking away, he or she should consider two things.

1: Was an Indemnity Guarantee Premium (IGP) paid when the mortgage was first taken out. An IGP is often attached to a loan agreement providing insurance against the value of the property falling to a level lower than the mortgage (negative equity) and is designed to cover that difference, meaning the borrower doesn't have to pay it back when they move. Sometimes this insurance is included in the mortgage without a borrower realising so it needs to be asked about as it could mean a borrower can avoid being responsible for any shortfall.

2: The second thing to consider is remaining in the property for as long as possible, i.e. until the week before eviction. What is the point of leaving a property empty for a lender to sort out, when a borrower could still be living there trying to negotiate an agreement with their lender. Walking away and attempting to forget about a repossessed home does not benefit a borrower in any way.

But even if mortgage payments during this period are not being paid at all, the end result will be the same. A property will be repossessed and any missed mortgage payments will be added to the total balance of the loan whether a borrower has been living in the property or not, so they might as well be as it doesn't make the resulting debt any less by leaving it empty.

Use this time wisely. It is a good time to be corresponding to other creditors and get agreements in place before you have to move and start providing a new address. Once you have a small agreement in place, even if it is £5 to a credit card company, they are unlikely to contact you again unless you fail to make a payment. But what they will do is credit blacklist you at the current (and soon to be previous) address.

In other words, don't walk away – make them evict you. Three more missed mortgage or rent payments won't make much difference to your overall debt. The indemnity insurance may cover this anyway and if not, any resulting debt will be included in the Financial Statement and dealt with like any other debt, with the offer of a long-term but affordable repayment schedule. Don't worry about it, and use this period as time to organise a deposit for a new home to live in and make a new start. Even when the housing market is strong, small business owners can still run into similar problems when business borrowings are secured against the value of a family property and the debt starts growing higher than its actual value. Anybody who has business debts secured against their homes should think about these options.

A court will rarely grant a repossession order where the mortgagee is making a genuine attempt to sort out his finances and is making regular payments. It will normally only happen if the borrower has paid nothing at all, made no attempt to contact the Lender and does not attend any court hearing. The 'Ostrich Method', discussed on page 11 of this book, is a common one. Unfortunately, a court has no choice but to grant a possession order to the lender in these circumstances as for all the court knows, the house is empty and the borrower may have even left the country.

If you don't keep in touch with all parties, possession will be given back to the lender as a formality. But if a court can find a decent excuse not to repossess a property it will not do so. If you have already followed the advice in this chapter, it is unlikely you will find yourself in Court. But if it is too late and the summons has arrived, you must attend. If nothing else, it will buy you a little more time. If you face being made homeless, there is more information available in the Community Legal Service leaflet entitled *'Losing your home'*, which explains your rights. They can be collected at the local Citizens Advice Bureaux and are available as a download from **http://www.legalservices.gov.uk/leaflets**.

2. Credit cards

Obviously, if you are in debt and unable to meet your monthly payments, then stop using them – but don't necessarily cut them up and destroy them, as they may come in handy in the future. Just put them away in a drawer somewhere and forget about them.

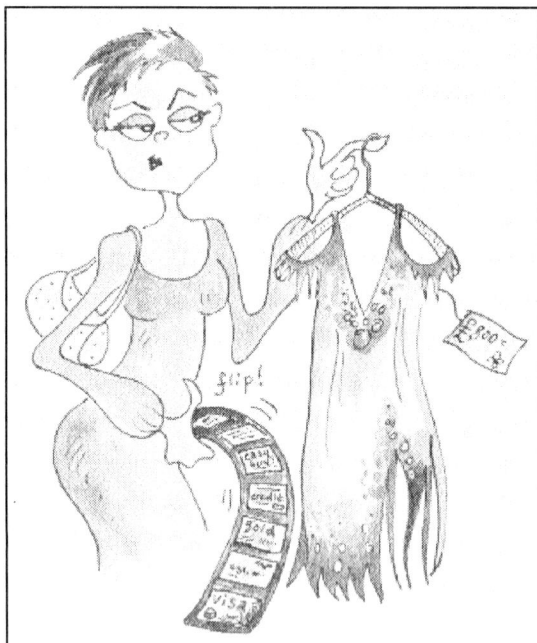

But if you are up to your limit, and unable to meet the monthly payments, write to the credit card company and explain the situation. Ask for the interest to be frozen on the account, make it clear you are not going to use the card again and offer a monthly repayment scheme. Using the Financial Statement, you can provide evidence of exactly how much you can afford and the card company will see for themselves that even court action will not benefit anybody. Therefore it is likely they will accept whatever proposal you make, as long as you can support your position with evidence. If you are overdrawn at the bank, then send copies of statements as the more information you can provide the credit card company the better.

Some companies will try to speak to you about it by phoning in the evening or at weekends and try to persuade you into agreeing more. People are actually paid to do that job. But don't be pressurised as, if you agree a repayment figure higher than your original offer during one of those phone calls and can't keep up the payment, it will work against you in the future.

Don't agree to anything just in order to get a debt collector off the phone. As these calls are always recorded just politely confirm that the position detailed on your financial statement hasn't changed and ask them to respond to the letter you sent in writing, not by telephone and never to telephone outside office hours again.

If you work during the day and do not want to give your employer's telephone number out, then make sure you refuse to do so. It's not unreasonable for you to insist upon this and if that means you are unreachable by telephone then that's how it is. If your credit card company writes to you, then as long as you reply, that is a good enough form of communication. After that, if they continue to try to contact you by telephone it could be regarded as harassment.

What if they refuse your suggested repayment schedule? Well, they will have to take you to court and spend money trying to sue you. But as we know, armed with your financial statement and responsible attempts to come to an agreement with them, you probably will end up with the same repayment figure anyway. Even better for you, once a court judgement has been made, the amount is frozen. This will result in no more interest building up, which will happen all the time you ignore the problem hoping it will go away. Take positive action and get it frozen before you even miss a payment.

It is another case where taking the initiative will work for you. Asking for an interest freeze early on and a lower repayment schedule should work. If not, imply you won't pay anything and the company will have to sue you for the balance. In the unlikely event of a credit card company doing just that for the outstanding amount, it will actually be better for you than worse.

Letter to Credit card Company

Dear Sirs

RE: 12345678

Unfortunately, my circumstances have changed over recent months, and I find I am going to be unable to meet my credit card repayments for the foreseeable future. I won't be using it again but want to maintain a good relationship with the company, so I may re-use my account in the future when things change.

I am writing to ask you to freeze the interest on the balance, as any increase will only make things worse for me and more unlikely I will be able to resolve my current problems. I have worked out I am able to make regular monthly repayments of £xx amount and I have enclosed a copy of my financial statement which supports this calculation.

Please let me know if this is acceptable as soon as possible as I am keen to reschedule my finances quickly. If this is unacceptable, I realise the next step for you would be to pursue repayment through a Court, which I hope is unnecessary, but if so, I will have to start making arrangements for this possibility.

Also, please let me know if my agreement with you has some form of unemployment or sickness insurance attached to it, insuring my repayments.

Yours faithfully

In almost every case, the Court will regard your actions as sensible and responsible and will do all they can to assist a borrower – especially by freezing the interest, which stops the problem becoming worse. Credit card companies know this, but hope you don't. It is important never agree a repayment schedule with the company that leaves interest accruing. There is no point in making payments of £20 per month, when the interest of, say, £11 is going back onto the balance. Don't be pushed, don't be bullied and stick to your Financial Statement.

Finally, a credit card debt is an unsecured debt. When the company gave you a card, they took a risk and, like every other creditor of unsecured debt, they will end up having to accept your terms. Do not in any way be persuaded to turn that debt into a secured one. There are several ways. One is they could ask for a charge on your property in return for a very low repayment and that should be refused. Secondly, they may try to persuade you into a taking a consolidation loan. They are widely advertised as reducing your debts into one manageable repayment and many card companies now offer these loans. They should also be avoided. Thirdly, some people may be tempted to re-mortgage their homes for the overall amount of several small debts in order to pay them all off in one go. This amounts to the same thing as securing the loan and should always be avoided. Do not be tempted to borrow money against the security of your home in order to pay off unsecured debts. You don't have to, so don't do it.

There are several reasons why not to do any of these things.

1. If the debt is unsecured, you hold the advantage, not the credit card company. They cannot force any repayment if you do not have the money to make a repayment with.

2. Consolidation Loans secured against your property means they can ask a court to repossess your home and reclaim their debt at any point in the future if you don't meet the new agreed repayments, and that gives the card company a major advantage.

3. If you stand your ground and force them into agreeing a small monthly repayment schedule, they will forget all about you. It gives you the opportunity of going back to the company in a year or so and informing them you have come into some money and want to make a small one off payment to clear the debt altogether. Many companies will accept a one off payment of considerably lower than the full balance, rather than continue having the larger debt being paid off at an interest free rate £5 per month for 30 years or so. But you will not be able to make such an offer, and clear the debt completely at a later date if the loan is consolidated or secured against your property.

4. Finally, some Credit Card companies, especially Gold and Platinum ones, have built in unemployment and sickness insurance attached to them. If you are sick or have become unemployed, you may find yourself drawing up to £1,000 in insurance payments for a year, clearing your card debt.

3. Bailiffs

Some Credit card companies employ private bailiffs. Most are both registered and certified and carry fancy looking documents and ID cards. But they also carry very little authority. Their official looking identifications cards and paperwork are designed to intimidate. They state things like they have been sent by the court, which they will do if you have ignored things and have been taken to court. Often they have been sent by the card company after the court case.

They usually guess you have little or no knowledge of procedure and will try to insist on removing goods to repay debts. They expect their fancy card will get them into your house. Don't let them, under any circumstance. Read this chapter carefully.

Bailiffs who are sent, including if they are sent by a court, who say they have W to seize goods to cover outstanding debt, have **no right of entry to your home**. They know this, and will employ dubious tactics to try to gain access. First, they will ask if they can come in, assuring you they are not there to remove anything, just to discuss a way of helping you avoid that. **Don't let them in.**

They might start talking loudly, in the hope that the thought of your neighbours hearing what they say, will lead to you letting them in. It usually works. Don't let them in. Tell them instead if they alert anyone else to your problem with this debt, you will call the police. That will stop them. Bailiffs publicising your debt by word and mouth (in this case by someone overhearing him) is as bad as pinning your name up in the Town Hall. It's not allowed, it's illegal and it's called **harassment**. Warn them, and they will leave with nothing but a message to their boss that they nearly got his firm in trouble with the Police for harassment. They don't want that.

Some good may even come of it. Victory in a harassment case is surprisingly easy and both the bailiff, and your creditor will be so embarrassed by this they may even write off your debt altogether.

What happens if you let them in?

Well, once inside,they are within their rights to take what is known as 'walk-in possession'. This means they are able to take a list of the goods they want to remove, even if you don't realise it, and will give you a further 21 days to pay up.

The problem with 'walk-in possession' is that is it as good as your agreeing to them taking your things. If you don't pay up, they can force entry and remove them. Don't let them in, because if you don't, then they can't be sure what belongs to you and what doesn't. They can't just walk in and take a rented TV, or borrowed video recorder or whatever. That's stealing. If you don't own it then it can't be used to pay your debts. If they don't know what you own, they can't take anything. Simple as that!

Don't let them in!

In the summer, you may have your front or back door open. Some bailiffs just wander in, claiming you didn't hear them knock. Your surprise and fear of this stranger will be eased when he shows you his official documents to prove to you that he is not an attacker. However, expecting the worst from someone walking uninvited through an open door into your home, you will be so relieved you will probably agree to anything. **Don't**. Throw him out and call the Police saying there is man (or men) going around, walking into houses with 'official looking documents' and you are worried about him. That'll get him arrested until he can prove he is legitimate, which might not be easy. Then you can ask a Court for a restraining order preventing this firm frightening your family. They will never call on you again.

But there are some circumstance where they are able to force entry. Usually not for debt but when the goods they are seizing do not belong to you and a court has agreed they must be returned. Examples are hired TVs, tools and other equipment. Or in the case of eviction, if the house is rented or has a possession order. Arrest is another example. But never for not paying your credit card or other unsecured loans. Another reason not to let them become secured.

If you have been to court and lost, ask what your rights are. Make sure you know what the next step is and what your creditor's options are. You can be sure they will use them.

Finally, if you get an unexpected visit from a bailiff, buy yourself some time. Always ask to see his credentials and ask for a copy of the 'Warrant of Execution' He must have one and you are entitled to a copy. Tell him to leave it with you for a few days so you can check it out. Then contact your creditor with your Financial Statement and come to an amicable agreement. I know you haven't done this yet because if you had, you wouldn't have bailiffs knocking on your door unexpectedly.

4. Harassment

As a follow-on to that section, now is a good time to talk about **harassment**. There are strict laws protecting individuals and small businesses from the activities of certain debt collectors and creditors.

It is a criminal offence to harass a debtor and his family by threatening, or committing, acts of publicity, violence or criminal proceedings. It is also an offence to obtain money or goods by deception, or in this case, by pretending to have official documents which have no legal validity. It is also an offence to distress or humiliate a debtor. The days of the town stocks have long gone.

This means Creditors and Debt Collectors have specific restrictions placed upon them.

1   They must not advise anybody else of your position either by accident or deliberately. This means talking loudly in order to be overheard, leaving messages on answerphones, faxing you, parking vans outside with 'Debt Collectors LTD' painted on the side or by pushing demands through the wrong door, such as next door. If they do any of this, you are automatically in a very strong position. They are breaking the law, and you haven't.

2   They must not wave around pieces of paper on your doorstep, or send you official looking letters which have no authority in law, but which imply that they have. This refers specifically to a large and well known firm of Debt Collectors who print all their letters to look like court documents. But they aren't.

3   They must not lead you to think you may be prosecuted in a criminal court for you debt. You can't. Even the age-old saying of 'I'll see you in Court' could in some cases be regarded as threatening and harassment.

4   They must not make frequent and unreasonable demands to a

debtor either at home or at work, which is likely to cause stress or embarrassment.

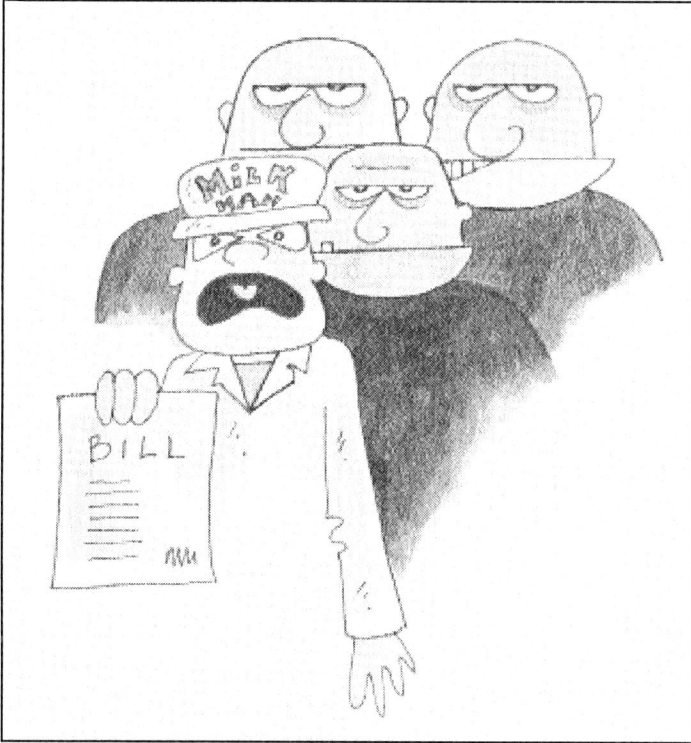

There are severe fines imposed upon debt collectors and creditors, sometimes even prison sentences. Recently, a landlord asked a colleague, who happened to be a big tough looking guy, to go and pick up his tenant and bring him to see him for a meeting to discuss two months' missing rent payments. At least that was what their defence insisted. The prosecution successfully argued the landlord and his 'debt collector' were guilty of kidnap and imprisonment (albeit for 15 minutes) The jury agreed and they were sent to jail for six years each.

It is also worth noting that anybody acting as a debt collector without a licence can be fined, and very often are, of sums up to £1,000. This means the local car mechanic, to whom you owe £500, who sends his mate round to collect it, can get into big trouble.

Creditors will assume you don't know about this law. As soon as they realise you do, they will leave you alone.

Most people are frightened of bringing prosecutions for fear of angering a creditor further, fearing they will become even nastier or immediately bring about court proceedings on you. Don't be afraid of this route. Even making a complaint to the Police will lead to a creditor, whether he be the local mechanic or an International Credit Card company, backing off completely. And how good will their positions be if they do eventually take you to court to try to get their money back. They will have no chance at all of winning their case. If someone threatens or harasses you, however minor it may seem, complain in writing to the Police and send a copy to your creditor. That will stop them.

If it gets any worse, ask the Police to take action. Almost all cases of this nature result in a conviction. You could offer to drop the charges in return for the debt being cleared. What more could you ask for.

Fact: Harassment is a criminal offence under section 40 of the Administration of Justice ACT 1970. Use it to your advantage.

5. Winning the court case

If you have used the information in this
this book, you should not be finding
yourself in court. But if it's too late, and
a date is set for a hearing, then there is
only one way to win the case, and that's
by attending.

Fully prepared, as outlined earlier, the
first thing you must do is ask the
registrar to set a 'protected earnings
level' which will cover all the payments
shown in the Financial Statement. This
means, for example, that if your entire
monthly budget lists expenses of £1000,
the court will allow you to earn that
amount before they are prepared to
make any judgement for any new creditor. This will mean, if you have
tried to come to an agreement with this creditor, and they have
rejected your proposals, they will end up with very little, or even
nothing. They know this, which is why it is unlikely you will be in
court if you have sent them your financial statement. Courts will
rarely jeopardise the agreements you have made with creditors who
were reasonable with you, in favour of one who bullied you all the
way into Court. A protected earnings level will ensure all those
creditors, especially the important ones like your landlord or
mortgage lender, will get paid.

Prior to the court hearing, make sure you have a file, and prepare your
notes carefully. Take copies of the letters you have sent them with
your proposals. Take your Financial Statement and copies of
agreements with other creditors and take a diary of events, listing
every contact you have had with this company. Especially if they have
been phoning you at unreasonable hours and sending people to visit
and 'discuss' the matter with your. Especially take their letters to you.

If they are the sort of company who sent statements and reminders out twice a week, take them all along, as it borders on harassment. No Court expects you to have replied to every one, so don't worry if you ignored most of them.

The court hearing is not about embarrassing you. You are not going to get into trouble and in many ways you can't lose. The worst that can happen is that someone tells you that you do actually owe this money. But then you knew that, so it's a no-lose situation. You have one objective with the court hearing and that is to demonstrate to the magistrate you have made repeated efforts to come to an agreement with the creditor, and that you can only afford what you are offering to pay, even if it's only £1 per month. Don't be afraid of how low the figure is if you have demonstrated it is the absolute maximum you have available.

Don't forget this is quite common. It's not unusual for an executive to be made redundant and go from £40-50,000 per year down to the standard Unemployment benefit in just a few months. All of a sudden a £350 monthly payment may have to become a fiver if that is all you have available. How can a court instruct you to pay more if you haven't got it. That would just be creating more trouble for you, and more trouble for the court as you would have no choice but to break their court order. You weren't breaking the Law before you appeared before them, they are not going to put you in a position where you have no choice but to break it afterwards by being unable to meet payments set at the hearing, as they are obviously unmanageable. They just won't do it.

A creditor refusing your proposals is not going to get a higher repayment by taking you to court. They might threaten to and for the small price of a court hearing they may even apply for one.

Fact: Many people will suddenly come up with the money on the eve of a court hearing, by borrowing it elsewhere in order to pay off the one creditor that has been giving them sleepless nights. Don't do it ...

they won't win. The courts know this and all that will happen is they will been seen by the court as the unreasonable bully they are. The creditor knows this and will ask to see you privately in a small waiting room to 'try to sort the matter out amicably'. By this time they will try to keep you out of the court room as they know the magistrate will not be impressed by them. What they want is to go straight into the magistrate and inform him or her that they have settled the matter and want the court to approve it. The court asks you if you agree and off you go, that's the end of that.

But in this small side room he will try to get more out of you than you can afford to offer. You have two options here.

1   Hold firm on your financial statement. There is nothing he can do about it and at this point, not in front of a magistrate, he has no rights to any of your financial information. Everything you have given them so far has been voluntarily, so tell him now to take it or leave it, without negotiation.

2   Don't even go into the room. Just tell the court usher you have had enough harassment from this firm and want the court to see the situation for themselves.

Fact: In some cases, a creditor will take it right to the wire and then accept your proposal at the last minute.

> One court agreed a repayment schedule of £5 per month to a car finance company on a loan outstanding of £4,500. It was going to take 75 years to pay off, and the interest was frozen, and he got to keep the car.

Fact: It is worth remembering that some finance companies cannot repossess a vehicle or other equipment if more than 30% of the agreement has already been repaid. They don't want you to know that and aren't about to tell you, so check your finance agreement yourself.

That lucky chap went back to the finance company a year (and £60) later and explained he had won some money on a horse race and wanted to offer £1000 in full and final settlement, on the condition the County Court Judgement against him was lifted and marked as satisfied. It was important he told them it was winnings, as if they had thought his circumstances had changed, or he had come into some money, they may have wanted to check. But they accepted his story and had a decision to make. It was either accept that or another 74 years at £5 per month. They accepted.

Don't be embarrassed about laying your financial hardship out in front of a court. They see it all day long and know what goes on. As long as you tell the truth in there, it will go your way.

6. Interest rates

All interest rates must be clearly stated on any agreement, by law. Normally this is covered by the standard application forms but not always. If, for example, you can prove you bought a computer on 0% finance, that was priced £1000 more than an equivalent computer in another shop where you could buy it outright, then that could be considered an offence. That is because the extra £1000 may be regarded as interest, or the arrangement fees of a 0% finance agreement.

If you bought a £100 washing machine on credit from a local second hand shop, and agree a flat rate or interest of 10% then the total you will owe for 'borrowing' £100 from the shop is £110. But you don't owe them that all year. After six months, you only owe them £55 but will still be paying the same interest on the original £100. You are being cheated.

It is for this reason that most reputable companies quote an APR Interest rate, which is the final interest rate on all fixed loan or hire purchase agreements. If the interest rate is not shown as an APR then you are probably paying too much, and they are committing an offence. Check your agreements.

7. Writing off a debt

There are several circumstances in which you can have your debt written off completely. You can be free of it forever. These circumstances entirely depend upon your personal circumstances. Creditors are generally reluctant to do it, although many will if they realise they have no hope of having the debt repaid.

1 If you become unemployed and are unlikely to find work again because of age, illness, disability or unusually high rates of unemployment such as being a miner in a pit town after the pit has closed down.

2 If you are part of a joint agreement, and the main earner dies. A lender may decide not to pursue the surviving borrower as he or she may simply be unable to afford the repayments alone.

3 If you are unable to work for a number of years for a genuine reason, such as becoming a single parent.

Fact: loans made verbally, such as those from friends or family members, still need consent in writing before you can regard them as written off. Verbal loan agreements are enforceable in court

Should you be imprisoned for non-payment of a Court Order, for debts such as Council Tax, VAT or Income Tax, you are not necessarily absolved of the debt upon your release. Prison is a punishment for breaking the Court Order, not a replacement for the debt. However, it is highly likely the debt will be written off if you remain unable to pay.

8. Little-known laws

Before you enter into any credit agreement you must have been given the following details:

1   The cash price for the item you are buying or services you are obtaining when being offered HP or Credit agreements. In other words although it is costing you £12 per month for 24 months, on 0% finance, the cash price would have been £200 if you had paid upfront.

2   The actual yearly rate of interest (APR) and the total cost of the loan, including the interest. You must have been given in writing the exact overall figure you are going to be paying. In other words not just £12 per month for 24 months, but the total cost of the agreement is £288.

3   The creditor cannot just point to the actual agreement forms you sign as evidence of you having been given this information. They must have given you other notice such as in the offer letter, adverts, brochures, catalogues and even price tags on items in shops.

4   You must receive a copy of the credit agreement signed by both yourself and your creditor within seven days. If this is not done, a creditor may lose the right to sue you for repayment or the right to repossess goods. If you haven't had this copy within 30 days, the creditor is committing a serious offence.

All Credit Agreements you sign must include the following:

1   Full details of how and when you can legally cancel or withdraw from the agreement

2   Clear details of your legal rights relating to the agreement and what action you can take, including who you can complain to, if you are dissatisfied with any part of the agreement.

This detail is usually covered by statements such as 'Your right to cancel. If you have signed this agreement you will have a short time to cancel. Full details are available upon request', and 'Your statutory rights are not affected'.

All creditors, including credit card companies and mobile phone providers, would be unlikely to take any action against you should any of the above information not have been given to you, in advance. Often it isn't. Read the small print – it is boring but can solve many problems for you.

> There is an example of a man who was about to hand back his builder's van, rather than suffer the indignity of having it repossessed by the finance company who were threatening to do so. He read the small print of his agreement and found out that as he had paid off more than 30% of the total cost, the company were unable to repossess it. They knew that, but were hoping he hadn't read the small print. He had, and they were forced to agree to a reduced payment level from then on. He kept the van.

For more information about this you should pick up a copy of the Consumer Credit Act 1974. It can be found at any court, library or Citizens Advice Bureau. It makes interesting reading and it is surprising how many professional companies do not stick to the rules.

No creditor, or his representative (bailiff or debt collector) is entitled to enter your home without a warrant, and there are very few circumstances in which a warrant for entry will be granted. If you have followed the advice in this book, nobody will get a warrant to enter your home for an unsecured debt.

No creditor is allowed to advise anyone else of your debt. This includes leaving messages at places of work, or leaving notices or leaflets outside your door.

9. Voluntary Arrangements

Every individual or partnership is able to avoid bankruptcy by entering into a Voluntary Arrangement. It is possible, should your debts be so large that you have no real hope of ever repaying them, such as in the case of a failed business venture, that you can use the Insolvency Act of 1986 (amended again in 2000) to your advantage. Read up on it.

As each case depends upon its own set of circumstances, so cannot be covered in detail here, you will have to take advice from either a solicitor, bank manager or the local Citizens Advice Bureau. Most of your creditors probably will not have heard of a Voluntary Arrangement. It is easy to sort it out yourself as long as you read up on it, but you could also approach a licensed Insolvency Practitioner to arrange it for you. They will charge a fee, but in the case of very large debts, it is well worth it.

This is a brief outline of the process. Assume you owe eight different creditors large amounts of money:

Creditor	Debt
Midwest Bank PLC	£60,000
Fronder Personal Loans	£12,000
Credits Cards Ltd	£11,000
XYZ Personal Loans Ltd	£10,000
ABC Financing	£5,000
Fronder Computing	£4,000
Magazine Advertising Ltd	£6,000
Total	**£108,000**

Now that your plumbing business has gone down the pipes, or your bricklaying business gone to the wall, you will have no real hope of repaying that money. You are now claiming unemployment benefit and it may take the rest of your life to pay it off. Or will it?

If you declare yourself bankrupt, you will be relieved of many, if not all, of your assets and may well be restricted from replacing them in the near future. But you can apply to enter into a Voluntary Agreement with your creditors. It means you get them all together and offer to repay the court as much as possible, without being reduced to a penniless tramp in the process.

You may be able to demonstrate to your creditors that they will get more repaid this way, than they would if one or more of them made you bankrupt. You may be able to get away with a three-year agreement, after which every debt is written off.

It is possible, for example, that you calculate (by using your Financial Statement) you will only be able to repay £300 per month. And that three years is long enough to be saddled with this burden before you can move on. This means you will be paying back £10,800, or ten pence in every pound.

Creditor	Debt	Repayment
Midwest Bank PLC	£60,000	£6,000
Fronder Personal Loans	£12,000	£1,200
Credits Cards Ltd	£11,000	£1,100
XYZ Personal Loans Ltd	£10,000	£1,000
ABC Financing	£5,000	£500
Fronder Computing	£4,000	£400
Magazine Advertising Ltd	£6,000	£600
Total	**£108,000**	**£10,800**

NB: These figures are only examples. There are cases where only one penny in the pound has been accepted.

Make sure all your debts are included, however small. You might as well deal with them all at the same time. During the process, all creditors will be asked to vote on whether to accept your proposals or not. Those who fail to turn up to the meeting, and many of the larger creditors who already realise your position don't bother, lose their right to vote and have to accept the decision of the majority.

As long as 75% vote to accept your proposal, the arrangement will be agreed by the court. For this reason, make sure you are in contact with each creditor because some may agree to it and not turn up to vote. You may need their vote. If any of them strongly disagree, usually because they don't understand the process, then they are likely to be outvoted. There may be some that try to negotiate but if you haven't got it, you haven't got it. No creditor will agree to another getting a higher percentage.

If, during the agreed period, you come into some money by way of inheritance, lottery winnings or by writing a best selling book about your experiences, then you will have to pay that money into the court in order to reduce your debts. But once that period is over, that's it. Your slate is wiped clean and you are free from those debts forever. But if you try to arrange finance with any of these sources again, you may find them a little unhelpful.

For more details about Voluntary Arrangements, ask any solicitor, court or library for a free booklet.

10.   Bankruptcy

Bankruptcy is a serious matter, but even if you are already in debt, it doesn't mean you must declare yourself bankrupt. Bankruptcy is a way of freeing yourself from debts you cannot afford to pay and have no hope of repaying in the foreseeable future. It will almost certainly involve the sale or closure of any business you are involved in and the loss of any major asset you have such as a house or other property. There are also future restrictions imposed upon you so alternatives to bankruptcy should be considered first.

There are two ways to be made bankrupt

1. **By debtors' petition.** If you want to make yourself bankrupt you can contact your local court who will provide details of the nearest county court dealing with bankruptcy. You can apply for the forms and submit them with a deposit and small court fee.

2. **By creditors' petition.** Any Creditor who is owed in excess of £750 can raise a bankruptcy petition against you. They then present the bankruptcy petition at the High Court in London or at the County Court near where you live.

The court will then appoint either an Official Receiver or Insolvency Practitioner who will deal with the case and act as a trustee of your estates. The **Official Receiver** is a civil servant of the court who will administer the bankruptcy proceedings. He will fully investigate your financial affairs for the period before and during your bankruptcy and provide a full report for your creditors.

An **Insolvency Practitioner** must be licensed and is often an accountant or solicitor. They are responsible for disposing of your assets and paying off your creditors.

The Process

Firstly you will go to the office of the Official Receiver and provide all the detailed information regarding your financial affairs. Your prepared financial Statement will go a long way to help this process and the Official Receiver will inform you of exactly what other details he requires. Then, within 21 days of being made bankrupt you will be asked to provide a detailed list of all your personal assets, and of any other debt you have not included in the bankruptcy proceedings. It will also be your responsibility to submit all bank statements and records of your financial affairs, including any income or asset obtained during the bankruptcy process. You will have to stop using any bank or building society account and will not be allowed to apply for any credit (this includes using a credit card).

If you own your own home it may need to be sold and the money raised used to repay creditors. In some cases, however, joint owners may be able to delay the sale of any property for a considerable time and they should take up-to-date legal advice as soon as possible.

The Trustees will then arrange a meeting between yourself and your creditors to decide how much money will be shared out between them.

Once you are bankrupt, certain restrictions will come into effect.

- Firstly it is a criminal offence for a bankrupt to obtain credit of more than £250, either alone or jointly with another person, without disclosing the bankruptcy. This also applies to hire purchases and rental agreements.

- It is also a criminal offence to carry on with an existing business in a different name without telling those you do business with there is a bankruptcy order against you.

- Those who have been made bankrupt must also not either manage, promote or even start a new business without the court's permission and nor may they hold certain public office.

- New bank or building society accounts can be applied for but not without informing the company of the bankruptcy proceedings. Whilst applying, you must inform them you have been made bankrupt. After that if you are found to have more money in your account than is absolutely necessary for normal living expenses, your trustees can claim the extra to pay your creditors.

- Usually the period of bankruptcy is three years, after which you can be discharged (unless you have been bankrupted in the previous 15 years). If, however, you have failed to properly follow the bankruptcy instructions, the Official Receiver could order any discharge to be postponed. But once discharged, a bankrupt is usually released from most debts at the date of the bankruptcy. Some debts, including those accrued through fraud, criminal activities and fines are exceptions.

- Also, once discharged, any assets acquired prior to the date of the discharge may still be controlled by the trustees and used to pay off outstanding debts. But any assets acquired after the date of the discharge are not bound by the conditions of the bankruptcy and may be kept.

- Finally, it is possible to be made bankrupt more than once but a second bankruptcy order, after a previous discharge, may have more serious consequences. You may also be prosecuted if you fail to disclose any previous bankruptcy, especially if accruing new debts later.

More detailed and up to date advice can be found in the book *Bankruptcy: A Borrower's Guide* (published by Management Books 2000) or from:

The Bankruptcy Association of Great Britain and Ireland
01524 64305

DEAL WITH DEBT
in NINETY MINUTES

Assistance

5

Assistance

1. How to get free advice

The first place to start would be the local court. In reception, there are leaflets about all sorts of debt problems and they will always hold the latest and most up-to-date information. Libraries will also have information.

The Citizens Advice Bureau is another good place to find free assistance and they will even help you through the whole process. When you contact the CAB, don't start dealing with the first member of duty staff you can. Ask them who the debt expert is and make an appointment to see that person. Take away the leaflets, prepare for the meeting. Quite often, especially if it involves a court appearance, the CAB will provide practical assistance and sometimes even attend and represent you. They might sound old fashioned, but don't rule them out. The CAB is extremely well supported by ex-solicitors, retired bank managers and counsellors. They know what they are doing, and it's free.

Some firms of solicitors offer the 'fixed fee interview' which will buy you half an hour of their time, very cheaply. But make sure you are prepared and have specific questions as they may spend most of that time trying to make a proper paying client out of you. If you have a particular point of law you need answers to, phone the Court and ask them, or even write to your creditor asking them for the legal position. They will have to tell you the truth.

Free up to date advice

The Bankruptcy Association of Great Britain and Ireland – 01524 64305

Assists those needing help in bankruptcy, providing information and legal advice, especially to business people facing bankruptcy.

National Association of Citizens Advice Bureaux – 0207 833 2181

Provides advice, information and practical assistance on a wide range of topics including debt, social security, employment, housing, consumer complaints and legal issues.

National Debtline – 0808 808 4000

Provides a national telephone help line to help deal with debt problems throughout the UK.

Insolvency Helpline – 0800 074 6918

And the following websites are useful

Http://www.nationaldebtline.co.uk/
Http://www.insolvencyhelpline.co.uk/
Http://www.nacab.org.uk/
Http://www.adviceguide.org.uk/index/life/debt.htm
Http://www.studentloans.co.uk/advice/
Http://www.southhams.gov.uk/housing/Mortgage.htm
Http://money.msn.co.uk/life_events/debt/insight/tipsguides/Man
agingDebt/default.asp
Free Legal Advice – **http://www.venables.co.uk/individx.htm**
www.justask.org.uk, the Government's Community Legal Service
Directory
www.nacab.org.uk, the National Association of Citizens' Advice
Bureaux
www.lawcentres.org.uk, the Law Centres Federation
**www.fiac.org.uk, the Federation of Independent Advice
Centres.**

2. Free legal assistance

It is possible that you will qualify for legal aid, and this will mean you can employ a solicitor to deal with your debt problem. There is no harm in applying to a legal aid board. Any solicitor will give you the telephone number and address of your local branch.

The Law Society run a body called the Free Representation Unit (FRU). Young barristers will take your case and represent you in court for free. This forms part of their training and makes sense when you consider that they, like everybody else, have to start somewhere, and cannot charge fees until they are qualified. They might as well learn on the job. Contact the Law Society and ask them about the FRU.

3. Insurance

There are many loans, bank accounts, credits cards and other forms of finance now which provide insurance against non-payment. You might not even know you have it. Check all your agreements for insurance policies. Some bank accounts now even come with free legal advice. Check with your business or personal bank manager. You may find your overdraft covered by unemployment insurance and a free solicitor to deal with your other debts.

4. Stress and worry-free nights

Each and every subject in this book can be researched even further. The object of it is to demonstrate to you in only 90 minutes, which is the length of time it should have taken you to read it, that your debt problem, however bad it seems, can be resolved and will set you on the path of getting out of it altogether.

If there are any subjects, such as bailiffs or interest rates, that you feel you need to know more about, then go and research it and become your own expert. You will find the law and the courts very much on your side.

Having completed reading this book, you will know you have nothing to fear from a creditor or debt collector. No one can intimidate you now and you can deal with them on your own terms.

Once you have started this process of getting out of debt, you can look forward to the postman arriving again, as the chances are he is bringing good news, not bad.

Appendix

Administration of Justice Act 1970

1. A person commits an offence if, with the object of coercing another person to pay money claimed from the other as a debt due under a contract,

   1. harasses the other with demands for payment which, in respect of their frequency or the manner or occasion of making any such demand, or of any threat of publicity by which any demand is accompanied, are calculated to subject him or members of his family or household to alarm, distress or humiliation;

   2. falsely represents, in relation to the money claimed, that criminal proceedings lie for failure to pay it;

   3. falsely represents himself to be authorised in some official capacity to claim or enforce payment; or

   4. utters a document falsely represented by him to have some official character or purporting to have some official character which he knows it has not.

2. A person may be guilty of an offence by virtue of subsection (1)(a) above if he concerts with others in the taking of such action as is described in that paragraph notwithstanding that his own course of conduct does not by itself amount to harassment.

3. Subsection 1(a) above does not apply to anything done by a

person which is reasonable (and otherwise permissible in law) for the purpose--

1. of securing the discharge of an obligation due, or believed by him to be due to himself or to persons for whom he acts, or protecting himself or them from future loss; or

2. of the enforcement of any liability by legal process.

4. A person found guilty of an offence under this section shall be liable on summary conviction to a fine not exceeding level 3 on the standard scale.

Index

30% repayment rule, 101

Administration of Justice Act 1970, 123
Anonymous threatening letters, 51
Appearing in court, 40
APR, 104, 106
Arrears, 84
Assistance, 117
Assured Shorthold Tenancy Act, 49
Attachment of Earnings Order, 73

Bailiffs, 93
Bankruptcy, 109, 111
Bankruptcy proceedings, 112
Banks, 22
Benefits Agency, 67
Benefits for the low paid, 68
Bills, 15
Budget, 19, 70, 76
Budgeting, 12
Bullying, 37

Cancelling agreements, 77
Capitalisation of arrears, 46, 84
Car boot sales, 79
Car loans, 58
Cash price, 106
Change of address, 32
Charge on your property, 17, 91
Cheques, 73
Child benefit book, 47
Child Support Agency, 64
Child Tax Credits, 80
Children, 47
Citizens Advice Bureau, 117
Consolidation loans, 21, 91
Consumer Credit Act 1974, 107
Contact, 20, 23
Council Tax, 54
Council Tax Benefit, 55

County court judgments, 24
Court Case, 99
Court Orders, 18
Credit Agreements, 106
Credit cards, 56, 88
Creditors, 11, 13, 29
Creditors' petition, 111
Criminal offence, 96, 112
Cut-backs, 75

Dangers of ignoring creditors, 15
Debt Collectors, 96, 98
Debt list, 19
Debtors' petition, 111
Debts lower than £200., 18
Diary, 33
Don't let them in, 93
DSS, 67

Early settlement figure, 32
Electricity, 50
Equipment loans, 58
Estimated bills, 54
Eviction, 49, 85, 95
Existing debts, 23

Family fund, 70
Fast free loans, 10
Financial statement, 19, 30, 35, 52, 73,
    88, 99
Fixed fee interview, 117
Fixed repayment, 16
Free advice, 117
Free dental services, 68
Free legal assistance, 119
Free Representation Unit, 119
Frozen interest rate, 58, 88, 89
FRU, 119
Full and final payment, 37, 58

Garnishee Order, 72
Gas, 50
Grants, 67

Harassment, 89, 94, 96, 98
Help desks, 55, 68
Home, protecting your, 41
Household expenses, 17
Household services, 50
Housing Benefit Office, 46

Immediate Action, 29
Income, 67
Indemnity Guarantee Premium, 85
Indemnity insurance, 86
Inland Revenue, 78
Insolvency Practitioner, 108, 111
Insurance, 32, 120
Intentionally homeless, 49
Interest rates, 12, 19, 22, 104, 106

Judgement, 39
Junk, 79

Landlords, 44, 47
Law Society, 119
Legal aid, 119
Liabilities, 17
Limit your outgoings, 75
List of each debt, 15
Little-known laws, 106
Loans, 22
Locks, 49
Low repayment terms, 18

Mail redirection, 49
Medical prescriptions, 68
Meters, 53
Missing mortgage payments, 46
Money you didn't know you had, 77
Mortgage, 41, 84
Mortgage repayments, 84

National Debt, 10
Negative equity, 41, 85

Not taking a debt seriously, 12

Official Receiver, 111
Ostrich Method, 12, 86
Outstanding debts, 15, 35

Photocopies of bills, 52
Pile of invoices, 15
Pocket money, 70
Police, 94, 98
Pooling your income, 70
Positive action, 35
Possession, 49
Possession order, 48, 86
Private bailiffs, 93
Private landlords, 46
Protected earnings level, 73, 99
Protecting your income, 72
Purchase agreement, 58

Rent, 41
Rented accommodation, 46
Repossession, 46, 83
Reschedule, 16
Restraining order, 95
Review, 32
Right of access, 53, 93
Risks, 22

Settling out of court, 101
Six years in which to recover, 33
Social fund, 68
Solicitors, 117
Stress, 121
Stressful debts, 18
Student Loan Company Ltd, 59
Student loans, 59
Summons, 53

Tax Credits, 80
Tax rebate, 78
Time periods, 33
Trustees, 112

Unsecured debt, 23, 91

Unsecured loans, 22
Unsociable hours, 52

Voluntary arrangements, 108
Voluntary payments, 74
Voluntary repossession, 85

Walk-in possession, 94
Warning, 40
Warrant of Execution, 95

Warrants, 53, 107
Water companies, 50
Websites, 118
Working Tax Credit, 80
Worry of debt, 9
Worry-free nights, 121
Writing off a debt, 105
Writing to all creditors, 37